ONE HUNDRED
VOICES

The bronze pedestal of the Commonwealth Memorial. The relief image on top depicts aerial view of the Eighth Ward before its demolition. One Hundred Voices, No. 26-50

ONE HUNDRED VOICES

Harrisburg's Historic African American Community, 1850-1920

Edited by
Calobe Jackson, Jr.
Katie Wingert McArdle
David Pettegrew

With a foreword by
Lenwood Sloan

The Digital Press at the University of North Dakota
Grand Forks, ND

2020 The Digital Press @ The University of North Dakota

Library of Congress Control Number: 2020941984
The Digital Press at the University of North Dakota, Grand Forks, North Dakota

ISBN-13: 978-1-7345068-5-3 (paperback)
ISBN-13: 978-1-7345068-6-0 (Ebook/PDF)

100 Voices is an initiative of the International Institute for Peace through Tourism - Harrisburg Peace Promenade. The Foundation for Enhancing Communities is the official fiscal agent for the Peace Promenade's projects.

The research and publication of *One Hundred Voices: Harrisburg's Historic African American Community, 1850-1920* was supported by The Council of Independent Colleges Humanities Research for the Public Good Grant, generously funded by the Andrew W. Mellon Foundation; Messiah University's Office of the Dean of Humanities, Office of Diversity Affairs, Center for Public Humanities, and Department of History; and Highmark.

Cover Image: The main photograph on the cover shows Walnut Street near Fourth Street, Tanner's Alley, and Short Street ca. 1913. Now the location of the Commonwealth Monument. Source: Record Group 17, Series #17.522, courtesy of Pennsylvania Historical and Museum Commission, Pennsylvania State Archives, Harrisburg, PA.

Table of Contents

ZACARIAH JOHNSON 15 AMENDMENT
LEONARD Z. JOHNSON SR. PROFESSOR
WILLIAM JONES PHYSICIAN
HANNAH JONES CHURCHWOMAN
WILLIAM H. JONES PHYSICIAN
AGNES KEMP PHYSICIAN
MORRIS H. LAYTON JR. PHYSICIAN
MORRIS H. LAYTON SR. TEACHER
A. LESLIE MARSHALL PHYSICIAN

ROBERT J. NELSON STATE WORKER
CHARLOTTE NEWMAN HOUSEHOLD OF RUTH
LUTHER NEWMAN TEACHER
WILLIAM PARSON PHARMACIST
HORACE PAYNE TEACHER
CATHERINE PAYNE-CAMBELL TEACHER
ESTHER POPEL TEACHER
JOSEPH P. POPEL ABOLITIONIST

HARRIETT M. MARSHALL UGRR
WILLIAM E. MARSHALL PHARMACIST
WILLIAM H. MARSHALL TEACHER
JESSE MATHEWS PUBLISHER
CATHERINE McCLINTOCK UGRR
MILDRED MERCER MUSICIAN
MAUD D. MOLSON LECTURER
PERCY C. MOORE COUNCIL

Relief images of the Eighth Ward on the bronze pedestal, showing fire engine, train station, and Bethel A.M.E. Church. One Hundred Voices, No. 51-75.

Authors

Descendants are noted by a star.*

Ellis Anderson	E.A.
Olivia Bardo	O.B.
Sarah Becker	S.B.
Britney Brautigam	B.B.
Mary Braxton*	M.B.*
Christine Bye	C.B.
Hayley Cook	H.C.
Jean Thompson Corey	J.T.C.
Cate Cutting	C.C.
Chloe Dickson	C.D.
Molly Elspas	M.E.
Charlotte Splawn Glover*	C.S.G.*
Katie Heiser	K.H.
Famatta Hne	F.H.
Matt Jenkins	M.J.
Isabel Gonzalez	I.G.
Dylan Goss	D.G.
Haley Keener	H.K.
Nicole Kreimer	N.K.
Adriana Lima	Ad.L.
Amber Luster	Am.L.
Ashley Mathew	A.M.
Katie Wingert McArdle	K.W.M.
Sarah Myers	S.M.
David Pettegrew	D.P.
Joshua Reid	J.R.
Mary S. Williams Richardson*	M.S.W.R.*
Amalia Robinson	A.R.
Sam Rockhill	S.R.
Alexis Sheely	Al.S.
Ellissa Slader	E.S.
Janelle Soash	J.S.
Leiby Soto	L.S.
Isaiah Stoy	I.S.
Anna Strange	An.S.
Lydia Tamrat	L.T.
Annie Thorne	A.T.
Laura Cannon Williams*	L.C.W.*
Sharonn L. Williams, Ed.D.*	S.L.W*

Relief images of the Eighth Ward on the bronze pedestal. The Lincoln School and St. Lawrence Catholic Church are depicted in two buildings on lower left. One Hundred Voices, No. 1-25.

TO USWARD

Gwendolyn B. Bennett

Let us be still
As ginger jars are still
Upon a Chinese shelf.
And let us be contained
By entities of Self ...
Not still with lethargy and sloth,
But quiet with the pushing of our growth.
Not self-contained with smug identity
But conscious of the strength in entity.
If any have a song to sing
That's different from the rest,
Oh let them sing
Before the urgency of Youth's behest!
For some of us have songs to sing
Of jungle heat and fires,
And some of us are solemn grown
With pitiful desires,
And there are those who feel the pull
Of seas beneath the skies,
And some there be who want to croon
Of Negro lullabies.
We claim no part with racial dearth;
We want to sing the songs of birth!
And so we stand like ginger jars
Like ginger jars bound round
With dust and age;
Like jars of ginger we are sealed
By nature's heritage.
But let us break the seal of years
With pungent thrusts of song,
For there is joy in long-dried tears
For whetted passions of a throng!

Dr. Jean Corey, Lenwood Sloan, and students on the South Lawn of the State Capitol, the future site of "A Gathering at the Crossroads" memorial. Note the 100 Voices signs.

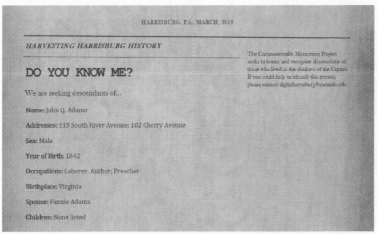

HARRISBURG, PA., MARCH, 2019

HARVESTING HARRISBURG HISTORY

DO YOU KNOW ME?

We are seeking descendants of...

Name: John Q. Adams

Addresses: 115 South River Avenue; 102 Cherry Avenue

Sex: Male

Year of Birth: 1842

Occupations: Laborer; Author; Preacher

Birthplace: Virginia

Spouse: Fannie Adams

Children: None listed

The Commonwealth Monument Project seeks to honor and recognize descendants of those who lived in the shadows of the Capitol. If you could help us identify this person, please contact digitalharrisburg@messiah.edu.

The original "Do You Know Me?" Cards designed by former Messiah history students, Rachel Williams and Mary Culler and directed to ancestors. These were posted on the Old Eighth Ward Facebook page in spring 2019.

FOREWORD

Lenwood Sloan,
Project Direct of the Commonwealth Monument Project

In normal times, each month, thousands of sojourners would travel down Commonwealth Ave past the dynamic Capitol fountain and on to Walnut or Market Streets. In addition, the Pennsylvania Department of General Services boasts an impressive 100,000 visitors a year who tour the Capitol Complex. Many of them are students experiencing the impressive grounds for the first time.

Let's add approximately 5.000 to 8,000 state workers, legislative staff advocates and lobbyists who descend upon twelve state facilities for their daily routines. That's a lot of people!

Whether they come as frequent visitors, day trippers, or tourists, most who traverse the area know very little about the proud diverse community or the Black enterprise that once wrapped itself around the Capitol's landmark domed building.

Today, there is not a single brick, cornice, door step, pillar, post, or cobblestone to remind us of the vitality of African American life that resonated there.

Recently, our history committee (*"history detectives"*) turned up an array of compelling stories about families who lived in the community that became the Old Eighth Ward. Soon, there were so many important narratives that we were sorry that we could not include them all.

The Commonwealth Monument Project recruited Calobe Jackson to construct a list of 100 names that reflected the Old Eighth like a crazy quilt. Calobe also served as principal historian as the history detectives and Messiah Univerity staff and students curated the list, and developed themes and clusters. They discovered some people who had only been sojourners in town, and some were who born in Harrisburg and spent their entire lives here.

As the Project progressed, it was evident that the new installation should inspire moments of memory and opportunities for reflection.

The design and history committees combined to explore ways to remember the people of the Old Eighth Ward through spotlighting the 100 names. The question of the day became, *"How should we honor a Neighborhood through the design and installation of a monument to the value of the vote?"*

Throughout 2019, our design committee collaborated with the team of A.R.T. Foundry Enterprise Inc to conceive and design the first African American monument to be placed on the Pennsylvania Capitol grounds. The multiple elements of the new installation honor the crossroads of the 150th anniversary of the Fifteenth Amendment and the Nineteenth Amendment's 100th anniversary.

Meanwhile, our fundraising and development subcommittee ruminated on a strategy to invite 100 citizens to each purchase a brick. Similar to a number of area monument projects, purchase of a brick would help support the funding of the new work. All agreed that the bricks should have the names of 100 Voices of the Old Eighth Ward.

Artist Becky Ault and her team all reminded us that we did no honor to the 100 names by walking on them!

A.R.T. Foundry reconceived the monument's elocutionist podium to create an iconic orators' pedestal. It now contains the names of the 100 Voices and bronze relief scenes of the neighborhood in times of prosperity. Upon the top of the pedestal is a miniature of the once valued now vanished neighborhood. Four life sized bronze figures of great African American orators stand around the iconic pedestal. The monument surface mimics the cobblestones of the old streets, alleys, and byways of the historic neighborhood. Still, we continued to ask ourselves,

"After the demise of the neighborhood through imminent domain, "where did the people go? What did they do? Where are their descendants now? Do they know their proud legacy?"

Following the passage of the 1850 Fugitive Slave Act, the Federal Bounty office was at 3rd and Walnut Streets for three years. It was one block away from historic Tanner's Alley, the gateway into the neighborhood. Interpretive markers near the site attest that the location was a well vetted site along the system of the Underground Railroad.

Throughout those three years, bounty hunters would flood the community with "wanted signs" describing elements of knowledge and bits of description about the person being hunted.

We appropriated the structure of the heinous wanted posters to search for the descendants of the Old Eighth Ward.

Messiah students flooded the system of social media to make connections. Students and history detectives have become completely immersed in the search for the descendants of the 100 voices. Each connection makes it more than a monument project. It's now a movement to join the Jubilee!

Between these covers you'll find what we've discovered through their incredible search. Finally, the team worked right up to the time to place the ink upon the page. In fact, they're still working even while you read this message. So, read all about it! Then let us know if you can help us find an African American descendant of the Old Eighth Ward.

The inter-generational discoveries of the 100 Voices project have been most rewarding. In this photo, the late Marian Dornell, local poet and great-granddaughter of Hannah Braxton Jones, stands with a young poet from Marshall Math Science Academy. The student wrote a poem about Hannah Jones through a Poetry in Place Workshop led by Messiah faculty and students. Photo courtesy of Dr. Jean Corey.

PREFACE

Calobe Jackson, Jr., Katie Wingert McArdle, and David Pettegrew

In 2020, a coalition of citizens, organizations, educators, and legislators came together dedicated to establishing a new monument on the Irvis Equality Circle on the South Lawn of the State Capitol Grounds in Harrisburg, Pennsylvania. The Commonwealth Memorial, titled "A Gathering at the Crossroads," features life-size bronze statues of four notable African American orators who resided in or visited Harrisburg in the later 19th century: Thomas Morris Chester, Frances Ellen Watkins Harper, William Howard Day, and Jacob Compton. They stand engaged in conversation about the successful passing of the Fifteenth Amendment in 1870 that gave Black men the right to vote while also looking forward (through the pose of Frances Harper) to the day when women would gain suffrage (1920). The speakers surround a bronze pedestal that features reliefs of the buildings of Harrisburg's vanished Old Eighth Ward—the vibrant multi-ethnic neighborhood removed in 1913-1919 to create the green space surrounding the State Capitol—and the inscribed names of one hundred men and women who were catalytic agents for suffrage, citizenship, and opportunity and betterment between 1850 and 1920.

One Hundred Voices: Harrisburg's Historic African American Community, 1850-1920 is designed as a companion to the new monument by providing a series of windows into the lives of the remarkable individuals whose names are embronzed at the Irvis Equality Circle. The book offers, firstly, a sequence of biographical flashcards that includes the most important identifying information—dates of birth and death, names of family members, places of residence, and occupations, among others—so that the monument's viewers may learn something about these individuals and their place in local and national history. The work highlights also their unique contributions, legacies, and influence as evidenced in their own eloquent words and active lives, and in the beautiful tributes that others left about them. Our aim in this book is not to provide complete biographies of the 100 Voices—a task well beyond our time and resources—but to highlight major aspects of their lives, give voice to their talents and passions, and record their unique contributions to civic life in Harrisburg specifically, and Pennsylvania and the country more broadly. Most of all, we hope that these windows will inspire you, students of history, to conduct your own inquiries, explore the primary sources, and learn from their examples.

The individuals celebrated in this book lived during a period of tremendous change in the social, economic, and cultural life of the city, region, and country. Their lives, individually and collectively, intersected with key moments in American and Harrisburg history which included, among others: the Fugitive Slave Act (1850), the Underground Railroad, and the final decades of slavery; the Civil War and incursions of the Gettysburg campaign; the emancipation of enslaved Americans (1863); the struggle for the vote that culminated in the Fifteenth Amendment (1870); industrialization; the City Beautiful Movement (1900-1915) and the demolition of Harrisburg's Eighth Ward (1913-1919); revolutions in transportation, World War I; the 1918 Influenza pandemic; the quest for suffrage that culminated in the Nineteenth Amendment (1920); and racial segregation. Every person featured on the Commonwealth Memorial experienced one or more of these key events, and a number—including John Q. Adams, James M. Auter, Josephine L. Bibb, Cassius M. Brown, Sr., Harriet M. Marshall—lived through them all. Consequently, one will find in this book resilient individuals who faced head-on the travails and injustices of American history: freedom seekers pursuing a life to the north of the Mason-Dixon line; abolitionists fighting against the most evil institution of slavery; United States Colored Troops veterans soldiering with their very bodies to end oppression; suffragists seeking the most foundational right to vote; educators championing equal and fair education for all; and physicians, moralists, and Christian preachers and Sunday school directors working for the care and improvement of body and soul. One will find also a great variety of engagements in a wide range of human occupations, from the educated professional classes to ordinary occupations, from mothers and fathers, policemen, and lawyers to foresters, musicians, poets, janitors, automobile mechanics, and business leaders.

This book contains, in short, a heterogeneous view of Harrisburg's African American community and those individuals who influenced and shaped it. While most of those honored in this book lived part or all of their lives in Harrisburg, a number (e.g., Gwendolyn Bennett, Alice Dunbar-Nelson, and Jessie Matthews Vann) only lived in the city for a short time, while several—Peter S. Blackwell, Henry H. Garnet, and Maud Molson Hughes—were not residents but had such strength of connection to the people, churches, and organizations in the city that they have been included. Likewise, most individuals inscribed on the monument were of African descent, but Agnes Kemp and Catherine McClintock were white women who advocated tirelessly for the rights of the Black community. What unites all these individuals, especially, is their committed advocacy for freedom, equality, and justice, and their contributions to the standing and life of African Americans—and, indeed, the political power of all Americans—in the later 19th and 20th centuries. With the orators and the pedestal of the Commonwealth Memorial, the book collectively creates a record of the capital city's significant African American community and its historic struggle for political, social, and cultural agency that culminated in the passing of the Fifteenth and Nineteenth Amendments.

We ask you, the reader, for two pardons at the outset. First, the length of cards is at times uneven, reflecting not simply the different levels of student research, but also the very real differences in the public profiles of the individuals and evidence for their lives in Harrisburg. We imagine this project as an ongoing one and we hope you will help us to fill in gaps and correct any errors that remain. Second, in trying to give voice to the celebrated individuals, we have opted to summarize the contributions and legacies of these indivudals by using the first person in the opening sections of each card and to make use of contemporary terms "Black," "African American," and "communities of color." We recognize that this is in some cases anachronistic given the racial terms in use at the time—"Negro," "Colored," and "Mulatto," among others—but we have decided to standardize in order to emphasize the legacies of the past for the present.

***

We have so many to acknowledge in the publication of this book. 100 Voices was a project of the Commonwealth Monument Project, an initiative of the International Institute for Peace through Tourism - Harrisburg Peace Promenade, directed by Mr. Lenwood Sloan and undertaken through the fiscal sponsorship of The Foundation for Enhancing Communities. The endeavors of the CMP in 2018-2020 included living history sessions, scholar talks, poetry workshops, poster and billboard campaigns, an original play, historical research and publications, digital projects and interactive maps, press conferences, a social media campaign, the quest for living descendants, and, of course, the work of sculptor Becky Ault and her A.R.T. team and architect John Melham and Associates, to create and construct the bronze monument on the Irvis Equality Circle.

The publication of *One Hundred Voices* was only made possible by the generous contributions and support of key organizations. At a moment when our country feels the dramatic effects of centuries of systemic and institutional racism, it is gratifying to find support in institutions committed to celebrating the dignity and value of the diverse historical African American communities.

We thank Messiah University's administrators, especially, for investing in this important work: Dr. Kim Phipps, President, and Dr. Todd Allen, Vice President for Diversity Affairs, for making racial reconciliation a priority work of the administration; Dr. Jean Corey, Director of the Center for Public Humanities, for providing funds and resources to undertake the research shared in this book; Dr. Bernardo Michael, Chair of the Department of History, for his tireless commitment to diversity work and the special donation of departmental funds for publishing this book; and Dr. Peter Powers, Dean of the School of the Humanities, for his most generous contributions to the Commonwealth Monument Project and the publication and printing of the *One Hundred Voices* books.

Several other organizations were essential in making this book possible. A Council of Independent Colleges grant program, Humanities Research for the Public Good, supported by the Andrew W. Mellon Foundation, funded Messiah faculty and student collaboration with the International Institution for Peace through Tourism during 2019-2020. Highmark provided a generous donation in July 2020 for the printing of several hundred physical copies of *One Hundred Voices* for distribution at the dedication ceremony of August 26.

The research of the 100 Voices involved dozens of individuals over the course of two years. As Calobe Jackson, Jr., has noted elsewhere (LaGrand and Pettegrew 2020: see below), the compilation of the list of one hundred important citizens of Harrisburg developed organically out of conversation between Lenwood Sloan, Calobe Jackson, and others in 2018. Former Messiah history students Rachel Williams and Mary Culler crafted the initial cards for all one hundred names in winter 2019 via the databases of the Digital Harrisburg Project and Newspapers.com. Drs. Jean Corey and David Pettegrew of Messiah University, together with project coordinators Drew Hermeling and Katie Wingert McArdle, undertook the significant endeavor over two academic years of directing student research as part of the Digital Harrisburg Initiative and the Student Fellows Program of the Center for Public Humanities. Two other historians, Dr. James LaGrand and Dr. Sarah E. Myers, contributed class projects to the effort through courses on African American History and Public History.

As our attribution and authorship page highlights, some thirty Messiah humanities students were involved in the work of researching and filling out cards in the 2019-2020 academic year! History students Chloe Dickson and Anna Strange, especially, Katie Wingert McArdle should be recognized for their work to develop the biographical template and to train students how to conduct research using Digital Harrisburg databases, Ancestry, and newspaper databases to collect reliable information about each person.

When the academic term ended with the project not quite finished, Sarah K. Myers, Librarian at Messiah University, heroically stepped in to complete the unfinished research of twenty cards, and Elisabeth Ivey worked with us to copy-edit and standardize style across the lot. The book's editors—Calobe Jackson, Jr., Katie Wingert McArdle, and David Pettegrew—fact-checked the cards several times against primary sources, revised cards to standardize style and voice, strengthened descriptions, and added missing information. We are deeply grateful to Dr. Bill Caraher for working us on the shortest of timelines to publish this work at the highest quality with The Digital Press at the the University of North Dakota

We thank several other critical collaborators who made this book happen. Our project's catalytic agent, Lenwood Sloan, inspired and encouraged us with a vision of making intergenerational connections between the individuals named on the monument and living descendants. Dr. Jean Corey provided considerable help at every step in the process, from taking on the 100 Voices as a worthwhile focus for her CPH Student Fellows Program, to undertaking research herself and locating relevant poetry for the book. Several other history detectives, Brian and Kim Williams, Jeb Stuart, and Barbara Barksdale were outstanding collaborators who made constant contributions to our knowledge of these individuals over the course of the year. In addition, Ken Frew of the Historical Society of Dauphin County kindly provided assistance in locating pertinent information, and the staff at the Pennsylvania State Archives as well as the State Library supported the work and made important discoveries themselves, including an incredible letter exchange between Maude Coleman and the governor of Pennsylvania advocating for fair housing in light of residential segregation.

Finally, the research of this book took on particular significance when the living descendants of the One Hundred Voices stepped forward to embrace the research. We were delighted when Dr. Sharonn L. Williams, descendant of Ephraim Slaughter, contacted us to share the findings of her Genealogy Working Group and to volunteer to write the cards for their own ancestors. Dr. Williams and GWG members Charlotte S. Glover, Laura Cannon Williams, and Mary S. Williams Richardson completed cards for Ephraim Slaughter, Hannah Braxton Jones, Mildred Mercer Cannon, and Daniel G. Potter. Likewise, descendants Ann and Mary Braxton provided relevant detailsand subtantial information for George H. Imes and Mary Braxton Roberts. In every case, the discovery of descendants sharpened our historical pictures, led to new discoveries, and showcased the continuing legacies of the important women and men who resided in Harrisburg between 1850 and 1920. The descendants are themselves remarkable individuals who have continued the ground-breaking endeavors of their ancestors.

Our hope is that this book will inspire interest in the 100 Voices to that descendants and students of history can help to expand, fine-tune, and amplify the voices of these catalytic agents of change in Harrisburg's historic African American community.

Resources

We invite you to learn more about the 100 Voices and Commonwealth Monument Projects:

Commonwealth Monument Project Website. http://monument-paus.com/

Digital Harrisburg Website, with primary resources for further study: https://digitalharrisburg.com/commonwealth/

David Pettegrew and James B. LaGrand, eds., "Harrisburg, Digital Public History, and the 'City Beautiful.'" Special issue of *Pennsylvania History: A Journal of Mid-Atlantic Studies* 87.1 (Winter 2020), featuring articles by:

Becky Ault, "The Commonwealth Memorial: A New Sculpture for the Capitol Grounds" (pp. 225-232) [available for free download]

Jean Thompson Corey, "Reimagining Harrisburg's Old Eighth Ward Through Poetry" (pp. 192-202) [available for free download]

Andrew Dyrli Hermeling, "*Look Up, Look Out*: Discrepant Stories from the Old Eighth Ward" (pp. 203-211) [available for free download]

James B. LaGrand and David Pettegrew, "Harrisburg's Historic African American Community: An Interview with Calobe Jackson Jr." (pp. 212-224) [available for free download]

Rachel Williams, "History and Memory of the Old Eighth Ward" (pp. 164-178) [available for free download from the PHA website]

Larry Robin and Lenwood Sloan, eds., *A Gathering at the Crossroads: For Such a Time as This*. Souvenir Newspaper. Publisher: Larry Robin.

The older part of the Eighth Ward east of the state capitol as shown on a map of 1901. Most of the 100 voices had some connection to this part of Harrisburg, either in their locations of residence, worship, or social life. The area between North Street and Walnut was demolished by 1919; the remaining area of the Eighth Ward between North and Forster was demolished in the mid-twentieth century.

Commonwealth
Monument

The boundary of the Eighth Ward overlaying a modern aerial photo of the State Capitol grounds showing the location of the Commonwealth Monument.

INTRODUCTION

Katie Wingert McArdle

Scholar-activist and theologian Cornel West writes that "To accept your country without betraying it, you must love it for that which shows what it might become. America—this monument to the genius of ordinary men and women, this place where hope becomes capacity, this long, halting turn of 'no' into the 'yes'—needs citizens who love it enough to re-imagine and re-make it."

The Commonwealth Monument commemorates the agency and perseverance of such citizens during critical decades within the history of the United States of America. One hundred individuals, active members of Harrisburg's Black Community during the 19th and early 20th centuries, are celebrated on the very face of the monument pedestal, where the names of the 100 Voices are etched in bronze. On the hallowed grounds of the former Old Eighth Ward, where many of these individuals lived, worked, and served their community, the Commonwealth Monument serves as a visible physical representation, not just of the buildings and structures of that portion of Harrisburg, but of the legacy of the wonderful human beings who lived there. Those human beings—particularly the 100 Voices—re-imagined and re-made the Old Eighth Ward, Dauphin County, and beyond. This booklet seeks to further honor the 100 by sharing some of their histories of cultural agency and communal activism. Indeed, the positive contributions of the 100 Voices cannot possibly be separated from their activist commitments to combat, and to assist others in combatting, systemic oppressions.

In the year 2020, we celebrate the 150th anniversary of the 15th Amendment, the 100th Anniversary of the 19th Amendment, and the 24th federal census. These critical aspects of our nation's governance were made possible through the dedicated work of individuals like those the Commonwealth Monument honors—our 100 Voices.

In the year 2020, we must lament, too. We mourn evident oppression and unabashed prejudice, symptoms of a global pandemic that is far from contained. We weep over the streets, neighborhoods, and entire cities dubbed "impoverished" and "bloody" by authoritative voices, in eerie echoes of hundred-year-old newspaper articles about Harrisburg's Old Eighth Ward. We know that in these neighborhoods, which many prominent politicians and journalists might dismiss or denounce, important voices speak and act in both truth and love. There are the Elijah McClains, who play violin for the animals at the shelter, and there are the Breonna Taylors, healing the ailing in their most vulnerable moments. Indeed, these individuals are not just victims of gross injustice; they are family members, musicians, healthcare providers, teachers, religious leaders, athletes, and far more than fleeting headlines and social media trends can capture.

Our grieving inevitably leads to interrogation. In an era stamped by police brutality, by murders committed in eight minutes and forty-six seconds, there is much to question. What is progress? Whose voices do we ignore? Whose lives matter?

Black lives matter, and that includes historic Black lives. Throughout the course of this country's history, some human beings have bravely and consistently advocated for the inalienable rights that their country has denied them. Harrisburg has been a thriving hub for these women and men. Without their work, the country that West writes about—an unfinished, metaphorical monument that must constantly be revised and re-crafted—could not possibly be as beautiful or just as it is today. We are indebted to these brave people for their honesty, audacious agency, and indelible hope.

These individuals—and the Commonwealth Monument itself —invite rich conversation. The monument portrays four orators— Harper, Compton, Day, and Chester—gathered around, inviting us to listen at the crossroads. Indeed, those who have contributed to this booklet have listened and learned. Through the Commonwealth Monument Project, we have explored the lives of our 100 Voices and discovered layer after layer of value. Each of the 100 Voices did not falter in their dedication to lifelong community contribution, despite attempts from local government to prevent Black Harrisburgers from leveraging their agency. Although a white society routinely attempted to silence the 100 Voices, still these voices strained and cried out with success.

The descendants themselves of our 100 Voices can perhaps best attest to that success. Throughout the research process, descendants proved to be the most valuable resources. Descendants have not only palpably—sometimes unconsciously—carried forward the spirit of their ancestors' audacious lives, but descendants have also often preserved their ancestors' memories. Perfectly preserved family albums and faithfully transcribed oral histories provided us with a sense of not just the life of individuals, but also the history and character of the active networks within which they operated: churches, political organizations, fraternal organizations, musical groups, and more.

Because of the impact of systemic silencing, however, the process of researching these individuals—especially those for whom no descendants have yet been discovered—has been immensely challenging. Within this booklet, we cannot possibly capture the full scope of the life narratives of each of these 100 Voices. As we researched men and women, we triangulated among numerous resources. *Ancestry.com* served as an excellent starting point for learning about the vital details of an individual's life, including birth date, marriage, death date, relatives, and places of residence. In order to discern these details, we accessed digitized federal census records, historic city directories, death certificates, marriage records, and more. Although these documents provided us with crucial details, they were far from consistent. Name spellings, ages, and dates were often riddled with inaccuracies. In some instances, we could not locate an individual on public records until late in life, as those who had been enslaved were often not accounted for by name on the census or other documents.

In order to begin piecing together a more complete picture of an individual's life, we next utilized *Newspapers.com* and *ProQuest Newspapers*, which allowed us to access historic Harrisburg newspaper articles that at times mentioned or featured our 100 Voices. *The Harrisburg Telegraph, The Patriot, The Daily Independent,* and *The Evening News* proved to be our most helpful sources. Over the course of many years, prior to the genesis of the Commonwealth Monument Project, Mr. Calobe Jackson, Jr., had forged a digital path for future Harrisburg researchers. Mr. Jackson had used *Newspapers.com* to clip thousands of newspaper articles, and we often re-clipped the articles that he had so carefully curated. In the spring, the Messiah University library kindly sought a free trial of ProQuest's *Historic African-American Newspapers* database, which allowed us to read Black newspapers that at times included accounts of events in Harrisburg or provided a richer sense of some of our more nationally-recognized names among the 100 Voices. As we combed through digitized newspapers, we in turn found property loan records; job, marriage, birth, and event announcements; event accounts; advertisements; meeting and organization summaries; election summaries; and editorial accounts with information about local news, gatherings, and town gossip. Perhaps the most valuable newspaper articles we found were the obituaries, which included significant details about individual lives and also provided a literary sense of an individual's life scope and community impact.

Nonetheless, despite the plethora of sources available to us, we still found that there were gaps in what we could find. Although historic local newspapers published and edited by white Harrisburgers are preserved and digitized, historic Black newspapers, published in Harrisburg, are harder to locate. Despite efforts on the part of Messiah University, the Pennsylvania State Archives, the Pennsylvania State Library, and many Commonwealth Monument Project partners to find one particularly crucial Black newspaper, *The Advocate-Verdict*, we had no success. *Our National Progress*, William Howard Day's newspaper, also never turned up. Along the way, we discovered several voices, including Peter S. Blackwell and George H. Imes, who had also published newspapers. Sadly, we could not locate these important records of Harrisburg's history, as accounted by Black voices. Additionally, we struggled to find images of many of our 100 voices.

These challenges were often most marked when we researched the lives of women. Messiah University student researchers observed, time and time again, that it was difficult to excavate complete narratives of the lives of our female members of the 100 Voices. Our biggest clues were brief mentions of women in newspaper articles related to various activist organizations. For example, one newspaper article about Annie E. Amos notes that, in a meeting of the Independent Order of the Daughters of Temperance, Amos prefaced her report on the organization's activity "with a very interesting address." What was this address? We do not know, and we may never know. We can look at some of the male members of our 100 Voices—William Howard Day, George H. Imes, John Quincy Adams, and more—and we can encounter some of their words. With women, like Anne, we get descriptions—but no words. Only silence.

Over time, though, we noticed trends in the lives of our female 100 Voices. In the Black community, women were not simply relegated to kitchens and parlors; in fact, women held seats of honor at the table of change. Those like Jane Chester, Catherine McClintock, and Harriet Marshall were leaders in a highly successful segment of the Underground Railroad. Others, like Annie E. Amos and Josephine Bibb, served as staunch leaders of temperance organizations and suffragist advocacy groups. Still others, such as Mildred Mercer Cannon, Hannah Braxton Jones, Edythe Fields, and Janie Blalock-Charleston contributed music and speeches to the community. The churches were led by women, too; Jones and McClintock both founded historic Black churches in Harrisburg, and other women, including Annie E. Amos and Matilda Stuart, managed schools within those churches.

When our researchers could find obituaries for women, we were overjoyed. One particular obituary resonated with our students and with me. Senior history student Anna Strange discovered an obituary about Annie E. Amos, written by John Paul Scott, another member of the 100 Voices and a prominent Harrisburger. I stumbled upon Anna's careful digital archival of the obituary while preparing for a poetry workshop for middle-school students. The obituary helped to make sense of some of the silences we had encountered. The woman depicted is far from silent or vulnerable; she is resilient and strong. Scott writes: "Should not her memory be held sacred? ...Through the blazing sun or drifting snows, through the rains or heated drought, when the men were lax or mourners wept, she was always at her church, and of her widow's mite, she always gave to God's cause to foster and advance."

This is just a small taste of what our researchers have learned as they have tread among silences and systemic vulnerabilities, only to discover the security, solidarity, and agency that many of our 100 Voices leveraged within organizations, churches, and activism. What our researchers have learned—myself among them—has been life-changing. When we researchers have paused to listen at this "Gathering at the Crossroads," we have heard echoes more powerful and beautiful than we could have possibly fathomed. Those 100 names etched in bronze each have stories behind them.

As you read each account of each individual's tremendous life and enter into this project, I know that you, too, will be changed. You are an active participant in this work—not just a passive reader. I urge you to celebrate what these individuals accomplished. I beg you to grieve for the oppression they endured and the selfless advocacy efforts for which they never saw fruit. I implore you to relentlessly interrogate the silences you find, in these stories and in your own life and to soberly ask yourself whose voices you value, and whose lives matter to you

At this crossroads in the history of our country, those of us engaged with the Commonwealth Monument Project gather to dedicate one monument, while hundreds of others will be taken down. Meanwhile, Cornel West suggests that this country "needs citizens who love it enough to re-imagine and re-make it." Our 100 Voices exemplified this calling and risked everything for it. After months of researching these individuals' lives, I have realized that, if I, too, do not follow that example, I have learned nothing from this work. May each of us who encounter these 100 Voices be convicted to learn from and follow such remarkable examples.

ONE HUNDRED VOICES

Lantern slide showing neatly-designed East State Street in the Eighth Ward ca. 1905. Despite the rhetoric of filth, dense habitation, and slums—terms used to justify the neighborhood's demolition five years later—the neighborhood was modernized and up to date at the time of its demolition, with a beautiful new state capitol, new street pavements, and refurbished buildings. Image from Pennsylvania State Archives, Manuscript Group 085, series m17. Photo by David Pettegrew.

ONE

John Q. Adams

My Contribution: I grew up enslaved in Virginia and was denied the right to formal education, so I taught myself to read and write. As a freedom seeker, I found safe haven in Harrisburg, where I settled and eventually wrote "Narrative of the Life of John Quincy Adams, When in Slavery, and Now as a Freeman." In Pennsylvania's state capitol, I served as minister at Wesley Union A.M.E. Zion Church and as Grand Master of the Grand United Order of Odd Fellows at the Brotherly Love Lodge. I also started the Prince Hall Masonic Home and Orphanage in Linglestown, PA.

My Legacy: After emancipation, I was an icon of the efforts in Harrisburg toward enfranchisement and civil rights, particularly in my role in 1870 as assistant marshal for the Fifteenth Amendment Parade in Harrisburg. I was a faith leader who served and preached at Harrisburg's African-American churches, and the church communities that I supported are still active in Harrisburg today. The story of my freedom, told in my autobiography, is one of many "slave narratives" read and studied today, and it still speaks to the sin and degradation of American slavery as well as the resilience of freedom seekers. You can find my narrative at the University of North Carolina's digital collection of North American Slave Narratives.

About Me: "No man in Harrisburg, white or black, was held in higher respect by those who knew him. He was at once proud and humble, upstanding in defense of his race and religious faith, but ever ready to submit his own views to the spirit of fair play his own righteous life led him to expect of others. It was of such men as Mr. Adams that Burns wrote, 'The rank is but a guinea stamp, / A man's a man for a' that.'" — *Harrisburg Telegraph*, January 13, 1917.

Full Name: John Quincy Adams • Birth Date: Between 1837 and 1845, likely ca. 1837 • Death Date: January 12, 1917 • Place of Birth: Winchester, Virginia; born enslaved, escaped enslavement in 1862. • Gender: Male • Race: Black • Places of Residence: 27 S. Front Street (1870), 213 S. Second Street (1876-1877), 115 and 145 S. River Avenue (1878-1882), and 102 S. Cherry Street (1885-1917). • Connection to the Old Eighth Ward: Minister at Wesley Union A.M.E. Zion Church; preached at Second Baptist and Capital Presbyterian Churches; involved in numerous organizations that met in ward. • Family Members: Brother: Aaron Adams. Sister: Sallie Adams. Wife: Frances "Fannie" Adams, married in Elmira, NY on June 21, 1866. Sister-in-Law: Nancy Stover. • Education: Self-taught in reading and writing, as documented in narrative. • Occupations: Hotel worker. Coachman. City agent for Our National Progress, published by C.M. Brown and edited by William Howard Day. Minister for Wesley Union A.M.E. Zion Church. Missionary. • Church Membership: Wesley Union A.M.E. Zion Church • Activism: Significantly involved with the Masons and Odd Fellows; connected to the Underground Railroad and gave the prayer at Harriet Tubman's funeral; a founding member of the Colored Protective League of Harrisburg and the Citizens Republican Club of Harrisburg. • Connections: William Howard Day, Joseph Thomas, John P. Scott, Josephine Bibb, James Grant, W. Justin Carter, James Auter, Dr. William H. Jones; Morris H. Layton Sr., Cassius Brown, Ida Brown, James H.W. Howard, James Stuart, William H. Marshall, George Imes, Joseph Popel, John Gaiter, O.L.C. Hughes, Joseph Compton, John W. Simpson, Charles Carter, Anne E. Amos, Aquila Amos, David Stevens, Zachariah Johnson, and George Galbraith.

A.M./J.T.C.

TWO

Annie E. Amos

My Contribution: My husband and I were impassioned abolitionists in Harrisburg prior to the Civil War and used our home as a base of support for the Underground Railroad. I opened a kindergarten to help provide educational opportunities for Black children in Harrisburg, and I continued educational services for children in North Carolina during the period of Reconstruction. I also founded the Independent Order of Daughters of Temperance, which sought to eradicate vice and alcoholism in Harrisburg and contributed to the women's suffrage movement. My work was so successful that even advocates in the white community sought my advice and wisdom on matters of temperance and suffrage.

My Legacy: I made my communities better through educational and moral improvement. I educated numerous children of color at a time when few school opportunities were available to them, and in that way, planted the seeds for a harvest of new opportunities. In advocating for temperance and the vote, I laid the groundwork for women to be involved in gaining civic rights and an improved place in society.

About Me: "For each moment of flitting time, each pulsation of the heart some lonely traveler of this mundane sphere loosens the grasp of the things of earth and sinks into eternity. Through one of the opened portals Sister Amos, with outstretched wings swept to a life where Jesus is, to immortality. Hers was a picturesque character, sturdy, independent, positive and aspiring.... In the outer affairs of human life she was an abolitionist and her husband, whose home was an underground station, was often beaten and at one time incarcerated for acts under the fugitive slave law.... She was a suffragist in her church and the women of the Zion church owe a debt of gratitude to her. Should her memory not be held sacred?" — *Pittsburgh Courier*, Obituary by J.P. Scott, April 1, 1911.

3

Full Name: Annie Eliza (Williams) Amos. Alternate first names: Anna, Ann. • Birth Date: ca. 1824. Born to a French mother and a Martiniquan father. • Death Date: 1911 • Place of Birth: North Carolina • Sex: Female • Race: "Mulatto" (1850-1880 Federal Censuses) and Black (1900 and 1910 Federal Censuses). • Places of Residence: 432 South Avenue, Harrisburg, Pennsylvania (1870-rented until death in 1911). • Connection to the Old Eighth Ward: Resident at 432 South Avenue, a building that served as a political center of the Eighth Ward near the famous Battis Corner; Colonel Strothers ran pool hall at 432 South, and several Black social organizations, including the Independent Order of Daughters of Temperance, met at this property; involved in the nearby Wesley Union A.M.E. Zion Church and the Sunday school program there. • Family Members: Husband: Aquilla Amos. Children: Maria L. Amos, Thomas E. Amos, Sarah A. Amos, George Amos (son - died), John W. Amos (son - died), Aquila W. Amos (son - died). Grandchildren: Eugene R. Wilson, Lester R. Wilson. • Education: None listed on census. • Occupations: Kindergarten Director. Teacher. Assistant Superintendent of Wesley Union A.M.E. Zion Church Sunday School. Secretary.•Church Membership: Wesley Union A.M.E. Zion Church; member of the Elder Street Presbyterian Mite Society. • Activism: Independent Order of Daughters of Temperance; Elder Street Presbyterian Mite Society; Garnet League; Women's Christian Temperance Union. • Connections: Aquilla Amos (husband); Jane Chester; William Howard Day; John P. Scott.

An.S.

THREE

Aquila H. Amos

My Contribution: I worked quietly to help African Americans by opening my home in Harrisburg as an underground railroad station. I was the grand marshal of an annual parade on August 1 honoring the end of slavery in Haiti.

My Legacy: I served with the 5th Regiment in the Massachusetts Colored Cavalry from 1864-1865 during the Civil War. The Amos name is remembered both in my work and in the work of my wife, Annie E. Amos, who championed and spoke for equal rights for African Americans and women.

About Me: My "home was an underground railroad station" and I "was often beaten and at one time incarcerated for acts under the fugitive slave law." — John P. Scott, *The Pittsburgh Courier*, Annie E. Amos' Obituary, April 1, 1911.

Full Name: Aquila Howard Amos. Alternate first names: Quillia and Aquilla. • Birth Date: 1823 • Death Date: January 1, 1874 • Place of Birth: Pennsylvania (1850 *Federal Census*) or South Carolina (1860 *Federal Census*). • Gender: Male • Race: "Mulatto" (1850-1860 Federal Censuses) • Places of Residence: South Alley and Spruce Street, Harrisburg, Pennsylvania. • Connection to the Old Eighth Ward: Resident on South Alley, near Wesley Union A.M.E. Zion Church. • Family Members: Wife: Anne Eliza Williams Amos. Children: Maria L. Amos, Thomas E. Amos, Sarah A. Amos, George Amos (son - died), John W. Amos (son - died), Aquila W. Amos (son - died). • Education: Unknown • Occupations: Barber. Domestic Servant. Served in the 5th Regiment of Massachusetts from 1864-1865. • Church Membership: Wesley Union A.M.E. Zion Church. • Activism: Home on underground railroad stop; grand marshall of August 1 parade. • Connections: Anne Eliza Williams Amos (wife).

FOUR

Roscoe C. Astwood

My Contribution: As a messenger, I was one of a select group of African Americans who worked in the State Capitol.

My Legacy: I participated in the Colored Voters League and worked in the Capitol as a messenger. My father was well-known in the Wesley Union A.M.E Zion Church and worked as a U.S. Consulate in San Domingo and France. While my father traveled and gained public notice, I preferred to stay close to my family.

About Me: A "marvelous father" and "a real home man." — Obituary, 1968

Full Name: Roscoe Conklin Astwood • Birth Date: August 28, 1882 • Death Date: July 1968 • Place of Birth: San Domingo, West Indies; or New Orleans, Louisiana (*Federal Census*) • Gender: Male • Race: "Mulatto" (1910 and 1920 Federal Censuses) and "Negro" (1930 Federal Census) • Places of Residence: 428 Herr Street and 320 Muench Street, Harrisburg, Pennsylvania (1891-1929); 5415 Haverford Avenue and 1625 N. 59th Street, Philadelphia, Pennsylvania. • Connection to the Old Eighth Ward: Resided in Harrisburg north of the Eighth Ward; attended church in the ward. • Family Members: Father: Rev. Henry C. C. Astwood. Mother: Alice Astwood. Wife: Lillian A. Astod (Higgins). Father-in-Law: Josiah Higgins. Children: Edna Astwood, Lillian Astwood, Carrie Astwood, and Roscoe Astwood Jr. • Education: Attended school in the Penn building, a white school, but later ordered to relocate to the Lincoln building, the colored school; father refused to send children to the colored school even though children lived closer to the Lincoln building. • Occupations: Messenger for the Department of Public Printing and Binding on Capitol Hill. • Church Membership: Father was a highly recognized pastor in the Wesley Union A.M.E. Zion Church and spent time as the pastor of Bethel A.M.E. Church on State Street. • Activism: The Colored Voters League • Connections: Reverend William Howard Marshall, James Auter, Denny Bibbs, Harry Burris, Dr. Charles Crampton, Walter Hooper, Robert Nelson, and Daniel Potter, Sr., W. Justin Carter.

C.D.

FIVE

James M. Auter

My Contribution: I served under nine chief executives of Pennsylvania as a messenger for the Governor's Office. I was an elder at Capital Street Presbyterian Church. I also advocated for the appointment of Edward T. Hooper as Color Sergeant under Pennsylvania's Adjutant General, who served as the first African American in this kind of position in Pennsylvania.

My Legacy: In acting as an honorable and trustworthy man, I gained love and respect and earned a positive reputation in the city. As a messenger for ten governors, I made friends with many individuals. I was also one of the founders of the Citizens Republican Club of Philadelphia, through which I helped to break the color lines in several official positions. With my help, African Americans of the Seventh Ward gained positions as the Recording Secretary for the Republican City Committee, policemen, and city councilmen.

About Me: "By his death also Capitol Hill is poorer by the absence of one of its best known and most appreciated figures." — Governor Gifford Pinchot, *The Evening News*, February 19, 1932.

Full Name: James Monroe Auter • Birth Date: 1848 • Death Date: February 17, 1932 • Place of Birth: Petersburg, Virginia • Sex: Male•Race: Black (1870-1910 Federal Censuses), "Mulatto" (1920 *Federal Census*), and "Negro" (1930 *Federal Census*) • Places of Residence: 1113 Rodman Street, Philadelphia, Pennsylvania (1880); 245 S. 14th Street (1900), 305 S. 14th Street (1910), and 114 Balm Street, Harrisburg, Pennsylvania (1920-1930); Petersburg, Virginia. • Connection to the Old Eighth Ward: As messenger to the governor's office, knew the Eighth Ward well; active community member in Capital Street Presbyterian Church. • Family Members: Brothers: Castine Auter, William Auter, and Gaston Auter. Wife: M1: Laura V., m.unknown-1885. Wife: M2: Fannie E. Weaver, m.1888-1930. Children: Jennie Auter Roche, Ethel B. Auter Snow, Alda H. Auter, Dr. Nelson H. Auter, Mr. James Auter Jr., Dr. Milton H. Auter, and Virginia H. Auter. Granddaughter: Frances Evans.•Education: could read and write according to federal census. • Occupations: Barber. Sailor in the U.S. Navy. Messenger for the Governor. Appointed title of Colonel. • Church Membership: Elder at Capital Street Presbyterian Church (*Harrisburg Telegraph*, August 21, 1931) • Activism: Harrisburg NAACP (treasurer); Masonic Home of Linglestown (first superintendent); David Stevenson Post 520 (commander); Citizens Republican Club (founder and president). • Connections: Jane Chester (host at wedding); Robert Nelson (co-worker).

7

C.D.

SIX

Frisby C. Battis

My Contribution: I was a strong leader and supporter of Republican politics in the Eighth Ward and greater Harrisburg area. My poolroom served as a social and political hub in the ward and functioned as a headquarters for Republican activity in the Eighth Ward.

My Legacy: I was a strong leader, a politician, and a businessman in the Eighth Ward. I represented the ward for many years as a member of the Common Council. My association with the corner of Short and South Streets was so strong that it became known as the "Battis block" in the early years of the twentieth century.

About Me: "He was a member of Common Council during the bicameral days in the late nineties, and conducted his politics in his poolroom where he also ran a pawnshop." — *The Evening News*, Obituary, September 1, 1925.

Full Name: Frisby C. Battis • Birth Date: January 1852 • Death Date: August 29, 1925 • Place of Birth: Pennsylvania • Sex: Male • Race: Black (1880 *Federal Census*) • Places of Residence: 1514 N. 5th Street, Harrisburg, Pennsylvania. Resided and ran businesses at 139 Short Street and 141 Short Street. • Connection to the Old Eighth Ward: Resident on Short Street for a significant part of life; Republican political leader in ward; poolroom and pawnshop served as a political hub and polling place for the Second Precinct of the Eighth Ward; served on the Common Council of the Eighth Ward in the 1890s • Family Members: Wife: Harriet Battis. Children: Forrest Battis, Paul Battis, James D. Battis, Justice D. Battis, Frisby C. Jr. Battis. Daughters-in-Law: Mildred (son Frisby C. Battis III), Ora M. • Education: Unknown. • Occupations: Poolroom Owner. Pawn Broker. Cigar Dealer. Republican Politician. • Church Membership: Likely Capital Presbyterian Church. • Activism: Politically active through Dauphin Social Club / Hastings Club, Republican Club (vice president), Common Council (Republican representative for Eighth Ward), Dauphin County Afro-American League (chairman executive and state delegate), Republican County Committee (secretary in 1892), Eighth Ward election committee (member and election judge, 1884). Played baseball and served as the team director for Harrisburg's Olympic B.B.C. • Connections: Joseph Thomas (city council), James Auter (Dauphin County Social Club), Harry Burrs (Dauphin County Afro-American League), Joseph L. Thomas (contemporary state delegate to state convention), Cassius Brown, Colonel W. Strothers.

An.S.

SEVEN
William Battis

My Contribution: I served as alderman of the Eighth Ward during the 1870s. After retirement, I owned several local businesses, including a grocery store, poolroom, shooting range, and restaurant, which all served as gathering places for individual and organizational advocacy for African Americans in the city.

My Legacy: I positively impacted the Eighth Ward and Harrisburg as a whole through my advocacy for justice as an alderman and through my activist work as a Black Democrat. I advocated for diversification of the Black vote beyond the Republican party, work that has certainly borne fruit in the 20th and 21st centuries of American history.

In My Words: "As my efficiency as alderman of the Eighth Ward might be impaired by reason of the publicity given to this charge if I should remain silent, I publicly deny my guilt of the offense charged and pronounce it false in every particular, and to have been prompted by malice and petty jealousy...The matter having now been finally disposed of, a sense of justice to myself requires this public denial of guilt." — *Harrisburg Telegraph*, July 30, 1875.

Full Name: William Battis • Birth Date: June 10, 1830 (Certificate of Death) or 1838 (census record) • Death Date: May 18, 1907 • Place of Birth: Pennsylvania • Gender: Male • Race: "Mulatto" (1850 *Federal Census*) and Black (1880 *Federal Census*) • Places of Residence: Harrisburg, Pennsylvania: 500 Spruce (1875-1876), 401 Spruce (1877-1878), 195 Angle Avenue (1880-1882), 501 State Street (1883), 913 ½ N 7th Street (business- 1884), 819 E. State Street (1884), 525 State (1885-1887), and 523 State Street (1888-1889). • Connection to the Old Eighth Ward: Resident and alderman from 1875-1879; store owner. • Family Members: Wife: M1: Nellie Battis. Wife: M2: Ella Battis. Daughter: Gertrude Battis. • Education: Could read and write. • Occupations: Alderman. Retail Grocer. Restaurateur. Shooting Range owner. Poolroom owner. • Church Membership: Unknown • Activism: William K. Alricks Club, The Central Blaine Club of Central Pennsylvania (hosted meeting in home for the Central Blain Club of Central Pennsylvania in 1880 in support of James Blain, Republican nominee for president), Pittsburgh Colored Convention, and the Cleveland Tariff Reform Club. • Connections: William R. Dorsey, James H.W. Howard, William Howard Day, Joseph Popel, George H. Imes, John W. Simpson, Jacob Compton, David Chester, Spencer P. Irvin, and John Gaitor, Aquila Amos, Ann Amos.

Ad.L.

9

EIGHT
Gwendolyn B. Bennett

My Contribution: I published poetry in Harrisburg newspapers, performed and served as an Honor Roll student while in the Harrisburg School System, and contributed to the Harlem Renaissance as a poet.

My Legacy: I was an important artist and poet of the Harlem Renaissance who was educated for a time in the Harrisburg School District. I read "To Usward," a tribute to novelist Jesse Fauset, at the now famous Civic Club in New York, an evening which many consider the launch of the Harlem Renaissance. I started an artists' support group that included literary legends Langston Hughes, Countee Cullen, and Zora Neale Hurston. My poetry is still enjoyed and studied today. I kept a scrapbook from my days in Harrisburg, which is still on file at the Schomburg Center for Research in Black Culture in New York City.

In My Words:
"Oh, little brown girl, born for sorrow's mate,
Keep all you have of queenliness,
Forgetting that you once were slave,
And let your full lips laugh at Fate!"
—Excerpt from "To a Dark Girl" by Gwendolyn Bennett

Full Name: Gwendolyn Bennetta Bennett • Birth Date: July 8, 1902 • Death Date: May 30, 1981 • Place of Birth: Giddings, Texas • Sex: Female • Race: Black • Places of Residence: 44 Balm Street, Harrisburg, Pennsylvania; 2 W. 120 Street, New York City, New York; Nevada Indian Reservation; Washington, D.C. • Connection to the Old Eighth Ward: Harrisburg resident during middle school and high school; knew members of community of Eighth Ward. • Family Members: Father: J.R. Bennett. Mother: Mayme Bennett. Grandmother: Madelyn Shaner. Step-mother: Marechal Neil Bennett. Husband: M1: Albert Jackson. Husband: M2: Richard Crosscup. • Education: Lincoln School, 9th grade (Harrisburg, 1916), Central High School (Harrisburg, 1917); Brooklyn Girls High School (1918-1921); Columbia University and Pratt Institute (1924); Sorbonne in Paris (1925-1926). • Occupations: Poet. Artist. Writer. Editor. Director of Harlem Community Art Center. Professor at Howard University. • Church Membership: Performed at Wesley Union A.M.E. Zion Church. • Activism: Key agent in the Harlem Renaissance. • Connections: Joshua Robbin Bennett (father) and Esther Popel (neighbor and contemporary).

S.B./J.T.C.

NINE

J. Robbin Bennett

My Contribution: I served as an attorney who represented many people and institutions of color in Harrisburg and Steelton during the early 1900s, including during the state's seizure of the Old Eighth Ward. I represented Frye Hotel when its owner was forced from the ward and the hotel license transfer was denied by a judge.

My Legacy: I leave the legacy of advocacy in Harrisburg's and Steelton's African American community. Wesley Union A.M.E. Zion Church still stands as a representation of my influence as president. My daughter Gwendolyn's poetry points to my influence on her education and development.

In My Words: "Whereas, the said paragraph is too sweeping in its scope; let it be resolved, that this convention do here and now declare this paragraph to be untrue." — J.R. Bennett, *Harrisburg Telegraph*, October 23, 1914, at the Pennsylvania State Baptist Convention in response to a written statement by an individual, who claimed that all African American Pennsylvanians believed Governor Pinchot to be their friend.

Full Name: Joshua Robbin Bennett • Birth Date: April 11, 1880 • Death Date: August 13, 1926 • Place of Birth: Giddings, Texas • Sex: Male • Race: Black (Federal Censuses of 1880, 1900, 1910) • Places of Residence: Giddings, Lee, Texas (1880-ca. 1909); Washington, D.C. (ca. 1910-1911); 153 Balm Street (1914) , 44 Balm Street (1915-18), and 21 N. 3rd Street (Business, 1917-18) in Harrisburg, Pennsylvania; 371a Queen Street (1919) and 64 Brooklyn Avenue (1924-1926), Brooklyn, New York City, New York. • Connection to the Old Eighth Ward: Wesley Union A.M.E. Zion Church (president in 1914). • Family Members: Father: Robert "Robbin" Bennett. Mother: Rubelia Bennett. Wife: M1: Mayme F. Abernathy Bennett. Wife: M2: Marchiel Bennett (m. 1914). Daughter: Gwendolyn Bennett. • Education: Attended Prairie View College and Howard University School of Law. • Occupations: Teacher. Stenographer. Attorney. • Church Membership: Wesley Union A.M.E. Zion Church, Pennsylvania State Baptist Convention • Activism: Wesley Union A.M.E. Zion Church (president) • Connections: Gwendolyn Bennett.

S.B.

11

TEN

Mary Ann Bennett

My Contribution: I was a female businesswoman in Harrisburg after the Civil War, who operated a successful chimney sweep business with my husband. I also belonged to an activist family involved in the Underground Railroad. My mother, Judy Richards, was so influential in our community that an entire neighborhood, "Judytown," near Third and Mulberry, was named after her. My husband, Reverend Edward "King" Bennett, and I were active participants in the Underground Railroad and assisted fugitive freedom seekers as part of a vast network of allies in Harrisburg based in the Wesley Union A.M.E. Zion Church.

My Legacy: I was devoted to self-improvement and improvement for those of my race. Through my assistance in the Underground Railroad, many people had new opportunities to live life in freedom.

About Me: Regarding Mary Ann's husband and home: "'King' Bennett was also an active agent of the celebrated 'Underground Railroad,' and many a poor fugitive was concealed in the houses at Third and Mulberry." — J. Howard Wert, *Harrisburg Patriot*, December 23, 1912.

Full Name: Mary Ann (Richards) Bennett • Birth Date: 1798 • Death Date: February 17, 1874 • Place of Birth: Virginia • Sex: Female • Race: "Mulatto" (1860 *Federal Census*); Black (1870 *Federal Census*) • Places of Residence: Third Street, near Mulberry in Harrisburg, Pennsylvania.• Connection to the Old Eighth Ward: Member of Wesley Union A.M.E. Zion Church.• Family Members: Mother: Judy Richards. Husband: Reverend Edward "King" Bennett. Children: Grant Bennett, Thomas Bennett, Mary L. Coleman (step-daughter). Brother-in-law: Aaron Bennett. Grandchildren: Charles Smith. • Education: No education listed on federal census records. • Occupations: Keeping house. Businesswoman. • Church Membership: Wesley Union A.M.E. Zion Church.• Activism: Involved with the operation of the Underground Railroad.• Connections: William "Pap" Jones, David Stevens, Joseph Bustill.

12

S.M.

ELEVEN

A. Dennee Bibb

My Contribution: I invested in my community and sought office to represent the Seventh Ward. I was chairman for the Booker T. Washington memorial service at Bethel A.M.E. Church.

My Legacy: After serving in World War I, I came back to Harrisburg and studied at Dickinson Law School while working as a patrolman. I composed the alma mater song for Lincoln University in 1911.

In My Words: *"And for thee with our might / We will ever toil / That thou mightiest be supreme. We'll raise thy standard to the sky, Midst glory and honor to fly."*
— A. Dennee Bibb, Lincoln University Alma Mater Song, 1911

Full Name: Alexander Dennee Bibb • Birth Date: April 12, 1887 • Death Date: May 3, 1934 • Place of Birth: Harrisburg, Pennsylvania • Sex: Male • Race: Black (1920 *Federal Census*) and "Negro" (1930 *Federal Census*) • Places of Residence: Harrisburg, Pennsylvania: 631 Boas Street (1920) and 606 Forster Street (1930) • Connection to the Old Eighth Ward: Resident. • Family Members: Mother: Josephine L. Dennee Bibb Davidson. Step-father: Jerry Davidson. Cousins: A.L Marshall, W.E. Marshall. • Education: Harrisburg High School, 1904; Lincoln University, 1909; studied law under W. Justin Carter and attended Dickinson Law School. • Occupations: Police Officer. Served in World War I with the 351st Field Artillery. • Church Membership: mother was an active member of Wesley Union A.M.E. Zion Church. • Activism: Ran as candidate for Republican nomination for the Seventh Ward; served as executive committee member on local NAACP; served as commander of Buffalo Post. • Connections: Josephine L. Dennee Bibb Davidson (son), A.L. Marshall and W.E. Marshall (cousin), W. Justin Carter (student), J. Steward Davis (fellow serviceman in WWI).
C.D.

TWELVE

Josephine L. Bibb

My Contribution: I was the oldest living member at Wesley Union A.M.E. Zion Church in the 1930s, having been a member for 68 years. I was a prominent member of the Household of Ruth and made significant speaking contributions to Harrisburg's cultural community.

My Legacy: I was an exemplar of women's activist work and a voice in the community, whether I was speaking at Wesley Union A.M.E. Zion Church or serving the Household of Ruth. Wesley Union A.M.E. Zion Church still exists today, thanks to my investments.

About Me: "Don't forget this evening to go to West Street A.M.E. Zion Church to hear the Sabbath school concert and to hear Madame Josephine Dennee-Bibb, one of the finest elocutionists of her race. If you hear her once you will want to hear her again. She can move you to tears or to laughter. In rendering the 'Black Regiment' she is truly eloquent and sublime and sways her audience at will." - *Carlisle Evening Herald*, March 2, 1894.

Full Name: Josephine L. Dennee; Josephine L. Bibb / Josephine D. Bibb; Josephine Davidson • Birth Date: 1849 • Death Date: March 31, 1936 • Place of Birth: Harrisburg, Pennsylvania • Sex: Female • Race: "Mulatto" (1880 and 1910 Federal Censuses), Black (1920 *Federal Census*), and "Negro" (1930 *Federal Census*). • Places of Residence: Hamilton, Ontario (early childhood); Pittsburgh, Pennsylvania (briefly during early 1900s); 514 South Avenue (1880), 113 Cowden Street (1892-1893), 503 Cowden Street (1910), and 109 Anna Street (1916-1936), Harrisburg, Pennsylvania. • Connection to the Old Eighth Ward: Resident, speaker, church, and political and social organizations. • Family Members: Father: Charles Dennee. Mother: Mary Dennee. Husband: M1: William H. Bibb (until 1894). Husband: M2: Jeremiah Davidson (1895-1936). Son: Alexander Dennee Bibb. • Education: Educated in Ontario. • Occupations: Dressmaker. Homemaker. Elocutionist. • Church Membership: Wesley Union A.M.E. Zion Church • Activism: Involved in Miriam Household of Ruth No.1, Judith Household of Ruth, Woman's Relief Corps Convention, A.M.E. Zion Sunday School Conference, Secretary of Pennsylvania Afro-American Convention. • Connections: William Howard Day, A. Leslie Marshall (nephew), Alexander Dennee Bibb (son), John Quincy Adams, Joseph Bustill, Jacob C. Compton, George H. Imes, James Auter, John W. Simpson, J.W. Grant, David Stevens, Joseph Thomas, and Anne E. Amos.

14

S.R.

THIRTEEN

Peter S. Blackwell

My Contribution: As a man of words, I used my printing press and voice to elevate the status and quality of life for African Americans. I jointly published a newspaper, organized Black voters, and served on the borough council of Steelton. I pushed for more home and business ownership by African Americans, and I organized a quality school for Black children.

My Legacy: As Steelton's first African American council member, I improved the circumstances of my neighbors through voting and education to foster more and greater opportunities. My early work with the Afro-American Republican League of Pennsylvania helped pave the way for the support of the NAACP in Pennsylvania.

In My Words: "I landed here [the borough council], and I pledged to them, as well as to God, that I would try to make good, in order that they might never regret that they advised me to come into this office as a representative of the colored citizens of this borough. I do not think that there has been a moment, gentlemen, of my association here that I have not tried to be for the best interest of these citizens." —*Harrisburg Telegraph*, December 24, 1913.

Full Name: Peter Sullivan Blackwell• Birth Date: April 1860 (1900 *Federal Census*), 1862 (1887 Marriage License), or 1868 (1930 *Federal Census*) • Death Date: July 7, 1936, Midland Cemetery, Steelton • Place of Birth: Harpers Ferry, Virginia • Sex: Male• Race: Black (1910 and 1920 Federal Censuses) and "Negro" (1930 *Federal Census*)• Places of Residence: 118 Adams Street, 116 Adams Street, and 218 N. 2nd Street in Steelton. • Connection to the Old Eighth Ward: Actively involved in Steelton's civic life and printed an influential local newspaper read by African Americans of Harrisburg and Steelton. • Family Members: Father: William Blackwell. Wife: Mary A. (Washington) Blackwell. Adopted Son: Arthur Blackwell. • Education: Storer College in Harpers Ferry, West Virginia• Occupations: Printer. Newspaper editor, Steelton *Press*. Grocer. Salesman. Steelton Third Ward Republican Club. Steelton borough councilman. Laborer. Steelton stone quarry.• Church Membership: Monumental AME Church, Allen AME Church. • Activism: Paxton Lodge, No. 16, Masons; Swatara Lodge, No. 19, Odd Fellows; Steelton Cyclones baseball team (secretary and manager); Afro-American Republican League of Pennsylvania (president); organized and chaired committee to welcome home Black men of Steelton after World War I; Steelton Third Ward Republican Club; co-founded Hygienic School, Steelton. • Connections: George H. Imes (co-editor at Steelton Press), Frisby Battis and Dr. Charles Crampton (fellow members in Afro-American Republican League of Pennsylvania).

15

S.M.

FOURTEEN

Janie Blalock Charleston

My Contribution: I was a female African American teacher and leader in Harrisburg schools. I travelled and read widely. I was married to two influential men of Harrisburg: publisher Layton Howard and Baseball Hall of Famer Oscar Charleston.

My Legacy: My legacy is all the young people whom I taught at the Downey and Wickersham schools. My work in city and state offices paved the way for more female African Americans to have high-quality jobs in these offices. After 100 years of life, I was a cornerstone in my large family and was loved by many dear nieces and nephews.

About Me: "Janie was tough and 'always had spunk. She'd set anybody straight.' Being active and useful lay at the corner of Janie's identity; she hated nothing more than idleness. Books were central to Janie's self-improvement ethic." — from remembrances of her great niece Elizabeth Overton in *Oscar Charleston: The Life and Legend of Baseball's Greatest Forgotten Player*, by Jeremy Beer, 2019.

Full Name: Jane Grace Blalock; Jane (Blalock) Howard; Jane (Blalock) Charleston. Nickname: Janie • Birth Date: September 29, 1893 • Death Date: October 27, 1993 • Place of Birth: Russellville, Kentucky• Sex: Female• Race: Black (1900, 1910, and 1920 Federal Censuses), "Negro" (1940 *Federal Census*) • Places of Residence: 213 King Street, York, Pennsylvania; 114 Liberty Street and 12 S. 16th Street, Harrisburg, Pennsylvania.• Connection to the Old Eighth Ward: Daughter of Martin Blalock, prominent pastor of Wesley Union A.M.E. Zion Church; school teacher in the community and active in social organizations.• Family Members: Grandmother: Margaret Williams. Father: Rev. Martin Luther Blalock. Mother: Betty E. (Scott) Blalock. Siblings: Margaret (Blalock) Marshall, Bessie Blalock, Martin Luther Blalock, Derwell Blalock, Rev. Charles Blalock, Mary Blalock. Husbands: M1: Layton Leroy Howard (d. 1918), M2: Oscar Charleston. • Education: Central High School, Harrisburg. Teacher Training School, Harrisburg (1915). • Occupations: Public school teacher and substitute teacher, Harrisburg School District. Transcriber, Recorder of Deeds office. Dauphin County Voter Registration Bureau. • Church Membership: Wesley Union A.M.E. Zion Church. • Activism: Wesley Union A.M.E. Zion Church Missionary Board; Leonidas Club; and Unity Social Club. • Connections: Layton Howard (husband), James H. Howard and William E. "Bud" Marshall (relatives).

S.M.

FIFTEEN
Mary Braxton Roberts

My Contribution: I was a well-known public school teacher during my brief time in Harrisburg. I was an instructor in the summer programs at the Twelfth Street Playground. I engaged in my community by attending church, instructing folk dance, and organizing concerts.

My Legacy: I was a respectable teacher in my community and the President of the Francis Willard Loyal Temperance Legion.

About Me: "The board...extended a vote of thanks for her efficient services as a teacher to Mary Braxton." — *The Evening News*, March 2, 1918

"Efforts are being made by Miss Mary Braxton, playground instructor on the Twelfth street recreation grounds, to obtain a concert by the Perseverance Band for the benefit of the colored folk." — *Harrisburg Telegraph*, July 31, 1915.

Full Name: Mary Catherine Braxton; Mary Braxton Roberts • Birth Date: 1890 • Death Date: July 2, 1920 • Place of Birth: Pennsylvania • Sex: Female • Race: "Mulatto" (1910 *Federal Census*) • Places of Residence: 422 Cranberry Street, Harrisburg, Pennsylvania • Connection to the Old Eighth Ward: Resident on Cranberry St. near Tanner's Alley. • Family Members: Mother: Martha A. Braxton. Brothers: Joseph N. Braxton, James E. Braxton. Husband: Robert R. Roberts. Son: Malcolm Braxton Roberts • Education: Central High School for Girls graduate. • Occupations: Teacher. • Church Membership: Second Baptist Church. • Activism: President of Frances Willard Loyal Temperance Legion; Women's Association; Music Social Literature Club; Chairperson of the Sponsors Committee; War Camp Community Service • Connections: W.A. Carter.

Ad.L.

SIXTEEN

Cassius M. Brown, Sr.

My Contribution: I served in the brigade defending Harrisburg from Confederate forces in the invasion of 1863. I actively contributed to Capital Presbyterian Church as a charter member. I contributed to the political well-being of Harrisburg as the associate editor and publisher of *Our National Progress*, as a constitutional convention representative, and as a common council member. I was very active in attending the Black conventions of my day along with Rev. Charles Carter and O.L.C. Hughes.

My Legacy: I was a fixture of Harrisburg's political, activist, and church circles, producing a newspaper with William Howard Day, investing in the future of Capital Presbyterian Church, and running a successful barber shop.

About Me: "The late Cassius Brown was a model of good citizenship. He lived with the honor and regard of his fellows and died loved and respected by all who knew him, a shining example for others." — *Harrisburg Telegraph*, August 8, 1921.

Full Name: Cassius M. Brown, Sr. • Birth Date: September 17/19, 1844 • Death Date: August 6, 1921 • Place of Birth: Harrisburg, Pennsylvania • Sex: Male • Race: Black (1880 and 1900 Federal Censuses), "Mulatto" (1850, 1870, and 1910 Federal Censuses), White (superimposed over the faded, original markings for "Mulatto" in the 1920 *Federal Census*). • Places of Residence: Harrisburg, Pennsylvania: 516 Walnut Street (1876-1878), 644 Walnut Street (1880-1883), 642 Walnut Street (1884-1886), 414 Walnut Street (Rented 1887-1902), and 267 Briggs Street (Owned, 1904-1921). • Connection to the Old Eighth Ward: Resident; leader of organizations • Family Members: Father: Thomas Brown. Mother: Wilhemina Brown. Wife (m. 1865-1921): Amanda Cornelia Grey Brown. Children: Singleton Brown, Howard D. Brown, Richard S. Brown, Charles Sumner Brown, Cornelia Brown Jenkins, Ida Brown Colley, and Cassius M. Brown, Jr. • Education: Attended school; trained in the barber trade in Lewistown, Pennsylvania • Occupations: Barber (1861-1891). Publisher and Associate Editor of *Our National Progress*. Assistant Sergeant-at-Arms at the constitutional convention of Pennsylvania (1872-1874). Member of the common council of Harrisburg (1890-1894). • Church Membership: Capital Presbyterian Church: charter member, Sunday School assistant superintendent, superintendent, ruling elder, clerk of the session, and commissioner to Carlisle general assembly. • Activism: Harrisburg Fifteenth Amendment Celebration Committee; Harrisburg Republican Party; Pennsylvania Equal Rights League; Charles Sumner Death Meeting Leader; Grand United Order of Odd Fellows; and Negro National Convention. • Connections: William Howard Day, Ida Brown Colley, George H. Imes, Charles J. Carter, John Q. Adams, William R. Dorsey, John W. Simpson, John Gaitor, William Burris, O.L.C. Hughes.

E.A.

SEVENTEEN

Ida Brown Colley

My Contribution: I was a dedicated teacher in Harrisburg for decades, an active member of the American Legion Auxiliary, and a committed leader in Harrisburg's education circles.

My Legacy: I continued the legacy of my father, Cassius Brown, Sr., in social activism and leadership in Harrisburg's educational arenas. I served as a leader in pedagogical innovation and a teacher in advocacy for African American schools in Harrisburg.

About Me: "Miss Ida Brown, who teaches a lower grade room at Wickersham, has originated a set of 'thinking problems' for her pupils, by the use of which, she hopes to raise the 'standard of intelligence'" — *Harrisburg Telegraph*, February 25, 1922.

Full Name: Ida E. Brown; Ida Brown Colley • Birth Date: November 30, 1875 • Death Date: May 4, 1961 • Place of Birth: Harrisburg, Pennsylvania • Sex: Female • Race: Black (1880 and 1900 *Federal Census*), "Mulatto" (1910 *Federal Census*), White (superimposed over the faded, original markings for "Mulatto" in the 1920 *Federal Census*), "Negro" (1940 *Federal Census*). • Places of Residence: 644 Walnut Street (1880), 414 Walnut Street (1900), and 267 Briggs Street (1910, 1920), Harrisburg, Pennsylvania; Cincinnati, Ohio (1927-1937); 611 Forster Street (1940), 1537 N. 6th Street (1959), and 269 Briggs Street (1961), Harrisburg, Pennsylvania. • Connection to the Old Eighth Ward: Resident on Walnut Street and Forster Street; attended Capital Presbyterian Church; taught in Lincoln School and Day School. • Family Members: Father: Cassius M. Brown, Sr. Mother: Amanda Cornelia Grey Brown. Siblings: Singleton Brown, Richard S. Brown, Charles Sumner Brown, Howard D. Brown, Cornelia Brown Jenkins, Cassius M. Brown, Jr. Husband: Edward Duval Colley, Sr. (m. June 11, 1927-September 13,1959). • Education: Central High School graduate. Student at Columbia University, Butler College, and Chicago University. • Occupations: Teacher at the Lincoln School, William Howard Day School, and the Wickersham Annex School. • Church Membership: Capital Presbyterian Church • Activism: Elliott Association, American Legion Auxiliary (vice president); Wickersham Teachers' Association (president). • Connections: Cassius M. Brown, Rev. William H. Marshall, Harry Burrs, Jessie Matthews, Charles Crampton, W. Arthur Carter, John P. Scott, Prof. Morris H. Layton, Leslie Marshall, Esther Popel.

19

K.W.M.

EIGHTEEN

Harry Burrs

My Contribution: I served an important role as a messenger and clerk in the Pennsylvania State Capitol building. I led numerous organizations and societies in Harrisburg and consistently advocated for African American rights and equity. I organized the installation of a fountain honoring Dr. Jones at the entrance to 12th Street Park. My mother was the first Black resident to own a house in Verbeketown in the Sixth Ward.

My Legacy: I was an essential worker for the State Capitol. My role as a messenger made me a trusted member of state operations while my activism and engagement in my community made me a leader of advocacy and political work during my time. My work as a political advocate and active leader in the Sixth Ward united Black Harrisburgers and cultivated a sense of resilience amid the community despite the ongoing displacement of many African Americans in Harrisburg due to the Capitol Extension Project. I was recognized as an outstanding leader even in my own day in the *Pennsylvania Negro Business Directory* published in 1910.

About Me: "Mr. Burrs' operations are of a purely local character, and he has succeeded in building up quite a large and profitable business." — *Pennsylvania Negro Business Directory*, 1910.

Full Name: Harry Burrs • Birth Date: March 25, 1877 • Death Date: December 6, 1958 • Place of Birth: Pittsburgh, Pennsylvania • Sex: Male • Race: Black (1880-1920 Federal Censuses), "Negro" (1930-1940 Federal Censuses) • Places of Residence: Harrisburg, Pennsylvania: 1430 Marion Street (1900), 1430 Fulton Street (1910), 1407 Marion Street (1917-1930), and 516 Calder Street (1940-1958) • Connection to the Old Eighth Ward: Active in organizations grounded in the Eighth Ward; participated in advocacy work alongside and on behalf of many Eighth Warders. • Family Members: Father: George Burrs. Mother: Elizabeth Franklin Burrs. Siblings: George W. Burrs and Lizzie Burrs. • Education: Harrisburg High School graduate (1899) • Occupations: Elevator Boy (1900). State Capitol Messenger. Capitol Clerk (1930). • Church Membership: Harris A.M.E. Zion Church (likely). • Activism: Dauphin County Afro-American League (President); Unity Lodge No. 71, Colored Elks (Exalted Ruler, treasurer, district deputy for Central Pennsylvania); Elliott Association for Colored Grads of Harrisburg High Schools (organizer and president, 1901-1910); Sixth Ward Social Club (host); Sixth Ward Casino Baseball Team (manager); and Lincoln Cemetery Decoration Day (orator, 1899). • Connections: Peter Blackwell, John P. Scott, Rev. William H. Marshall, Sylvester Burris, William Howard Day, John W. Simpson, and Dr. William H. Jones.

C.C./K.W.M.

NINETEEN

Sylvester E. Burris

My Contribution: I was a leader of the Harrisburg Colored Choral Society and the Burrs Orchestra, a clerk at the Harrisburg Club, a well-known violinist in the community, and a conductor of the Harrisburg Orchestra.

My Legacy: My role as a leading Black musician in Harrisburg made me an important contributor to Harrisburg's culture and society.

About Me: "Mr. Burrs, leader of the Burrs Orchestra, and head of the Burris Musical Studio, is one of the energetic young men of Harrisburg. For several years he has been clerk of the wealthiest club of Harrisburg and filled the position with credit and ability. He is a thorough musician and has organized an orchestra of twenty-five pieces. His studio is located at 665 Briggs Street, where he teaches vocal and instrumental music, assisted by his talented wife, Mrs. Myrtle Burrs." — *Pennsylvania Negro Business Directory,* 1910

Full Name: Sylvester Eugene Burris • Birth Date: February 5, 1882 • Death Date: May 24, 1948 • Place of Birth: Harrisburg, Pennsylvania • Sex: Male • Race: "Mulatto" (1910 *Federal Census*) • Places of Residence: 665 Briggs Street and 919 Ash Street, Harrisburg, Pennsylvania • Connection to the Old Eighth Ward: Resident • Family Members: Wife: Myrtle Burris • Education: Studied the violin under Max Blumfeid and Mme. von Bereghy • Occupations: Musician. Clubhouse Clerk. • Church Membership: Bethel A.M.E. Church • Activism: Harrisburg Colored Choral Society • Connections: Harry Burrs (Choral Society).

A.M.

The Pennsylvania State Historical Marker for the Underground Railroad at the former location of Tanner's Alley at Walnut Street. Construction of the Commonwealth Memorial site visible in background. Photo courtesy of David Pettegrew.

TWENTY
Joseph Cassey Bustill

My Contribution: I was one of the youngest and most significant conductors of the Underground Railroad. I worked hard to found the Harrisburg Fugitive Society, the Capital Presbyterian Church in Harrisburg, and the Household of Ruth of the Grand United Order of Odd Fellows, which I founded in 1847. I also was one of the first African Americans to instruct school in Harrisburg from 1850-1862, and I worked with Judge Mordecai McKenny to found Sunday school for a collective of churches.

My Legacy: I assisted freedom seekers in Harrisburg by supporting the work of the Underground Railroad, and my contribution is memorialized with a marker at the site of the former Tanner's Alley in the Eighth Ward. I served as an ambassador for Black education and activism in Pennsylvania and beyond. Capital Presbyterian Church, which I founded, still stands today.

About Me: "He was always a polished writer and convincing speaker. He unstintingly gave his time and talent to every good cause. He was the youngest member of the remarkable Underground Railroad, being only seventeen.... Like Paul, he was 'a citizen of no mean city' —a Philadelphian of the Philadelphians—and was able to add to its honor and glory." — Anna Bustill Smith, "The Bustill Family," *The Journal of Negro History*, vol. 10, no. 4. *Chicago University Press*, October 1925.

Full Name: Joseph Cassey Bustill • Birth Date: ca. 1822 • Death Date: August 19, 1895 • Place of Birth: Philadelphia, Pennsylvania • Sex: Male • Race: "Mulatto" (1850 and 1870 Federal Censuses), Black (1860 and 1880 Federal Censuses), English, African, and Native-American heritage (according to family history and *Harrisburg Telegraph*, August 23, 1895). • Places of Residence: Tanner's Alley, Harrisburg, Pennsylvania (ca. 1853-1863); 403 S. 6th Street, Philadelphia, Pennsylvania (1864-1874); Lincoln University, Oxford, Pennsylvania (ca. 1874-1895). • Connection to the Old Eighth Ward: Resident on Tanner's Alley; led Underground Railroad operations with William Jones; founded Capital Presbyterian. • Family Members: Father: David Bustill. Mother: Elizabeth Hicks Bustill. Wife: Sarah Humphrey Bustill. Daughter: Anna Amelia Bustill-Smith. • Education: Educated in the "best schools" of Philadelphia (*The Journal of Negro History* 10.4 (1925), 641). • Occupations: Teacher. Wigmaker. • Church Membership: Capital Presbyterian Church • Activism: Harrisburg Fugitive Aid Society (co-founder); Grand United Order of Odd Fellows (Grand Treasurer, Most Venerable Patriarch, committee speaker); Household of Ruth of the Grand United Order of Odd Fellows (founder); Pennsylvania Equal Rights League (leader of Philadelphia delegates); Fourteenth Amendment protest convention (presenter); American Moral Reform Society (member); Philadelphia Union League (Fiftheenth Amendment parade chairman); Banneker Institute (trustee); and Montana Agricultural Emigrant Aid Association (co-founder). • Connections: William Jones, George H. Imes, Joseph Thomas, John Gaitor, Josephine Bibb, John W. Simpson, William Howard Day, and Cassius M. Brown.

H.K.

TWENTY ONE
W. Arthur Carter

My Contribution: I served the Harrisburg community as a postal worker. I was a graduate of Howard University Law School and was involved in Harrisburg's education circles. I was also an artistic leader in the city and directed and starred in the production of *Hamlet*.

My Legacy: I am remembered as an educational success story from Central High School, a dedicated postman, and a talented lawyer. I made a difference as a national ambassador for the causes of African American Democrats.

About Me: "W. Arthur Carter... a well-known jurist and graduate of Central High School... was a former Harrisburg boy.... Mr. Carter had many friends in Harrisburg." — *Harrisburg Telegraph*, November 24, 1917

Full Name: W. Arthur Carter • Birth Date: January 1876 • Death Date: November 22, 1917 • Place of Birth: Maryland • Sex: Male • Race: Black (1900 and 1910 Federal Censuses) • Places of Residence: 324 ½ North Street and 141 Linden Street, Harrisburg, Pennsylvania • Connection to the Old Eighth Ward: Lived on North Street one block away from the Eighth Ward on North Street; knew the neighborhood through church and friends. • Family Members: Mother: Maggie A. Phillips. Stepfather: George W. Phillips. Wife: Maggie Quander Carter. Son: Harold Carter. • Education: Central High School, 1894; Howard University Law School graduate. • Occupations: Postal Worker. Attorney. • Church Membership: Wesley Union A.M.E. Zion Church • Activism: Colored Knights of Pythias; Elliott Association • Connections: Joseph Popel, Morris H. Layton, Jr., Steward Davis, Leslie Marshall, George Gaitor, William Marshall, Jr., Rev. William H. Marshall, Sr., Jessie Matthews, Harry Burrs, John P. Scott, Ida Brown, Charles Crampton, Henry Highland Summers, Luther Newman.

S.B.

View down Fifth Street from State to South Street. On left is the Hotel owned by Theodore Frye, which provided lodging for African American travelers from the 1890s to 1914. Attorneys W. Justin Carter and J. Robbin Bennett defended the rights of transfer of the hotel during the demolition of the Eighth Ward. In distance is the Corona Hotel, former property of William Battis, which was still providing lodging for Black travelers at the time of its demolition in the 1910s. Parson Drugs visible in distance on right at the Frisby Battis corner, the heart of Republican politics in the ward. Photo ca. 1913 from Record Group 17, Series #17.522, courtesy of Pennsylvania Historical and Museum Commission, Pennsylvania State Archives, Harrisburg, PA.

TWENTY TWO
W. Justin Carter

My Contribution: I was a prominent and successful Black attorney, the second in history following T. Morris Chester. I heard numerous early civil rights cases in Harrisburg and nationally. I was a founding trustee of the Forster Street YMCA and an early leader in the Niagara Movement and NAACP. W.E.B. Du Bois and other prominent national Black leaders served as pallbearers at my funeral.

My Legacy: I was a prominent figure of justice and equality in a city that was divided by the color line. I rewrote the state's workers' compensation law, fought for racial equality, and brought a national activism to Dauphin County. My work as a leading advocate for civil rights and equity remain evident in the Harrisburg YMCA, the NAACP, and Pennsylvania workers' compensation laws. Although the Dauphin County Bar Association initially rejected my candidacy due to my race, I was posthumously admitted in 1994.

About Me: "During his 53 years as a lawyer in this city, Carter held a number of political appointments and places of importance on a number of commissions." — *The Evening News*, March 24, 1947.

Full Name: William Justin Carter • Birth Date: May 28, 1866 • Death Date: March 23, 1947 • Place of Birth: Richmond, Virginia • Sex: Male • Race: Black (1900 *Federal Census*) • Places of Residence: Richmond, Virginia; Annapolis, Maryland; Washington, D.C.; 49 S. 14th Street and 1831 Market Street, Harrisburg, Pennsylvania. • Connection to the Old Eighth Ward: Arrived in Harrisburg in 1894; fought different cases on behalf of residents and businesses in the Eighth Ward, including the prominent Civil Rights case of Frye's hotel transfer during the demolition of the Eighth Ward; member of Capital Street Presbyterian Church. • Family Members: Father: Edmond Carter. Mother: Elizabeth Reyes. Spouse: Elizabeth Carter. Children: Howard A. Carter, W. Justin Carter, Jr., and Thaddeus Carter. • Education: Virginia Normal and Collegiate Institute (Teaching Degree); Howard University School of Law, 1894. • Occupations: Teacher. Lawyer. Assistant District Attorney for Dauphin County. Legal Counsel for State Unemployment Compensation Bureau. Secretary for Lieutenant Governor E.E. Beidelman. • Church Membership: Capital Street Presbyterian Church (trustee) • Activism: NAACP Committee of 100; Forster Street YMCA (Board of Governors); American Academy of Social and Political Sciences; National Geographic Society; Chosen Friends Lodge; Omega Psi Phi fraternity; Howard University (trustee); Berean Secretarial School (trustee); London Universal Races Congress (representative, 1911); Workingmen's Social and Protective Association (founder). • Connections: C. Sylvester Jackson, George H. Imes, W. Justin Carter, Jr., W. Arthur Carter, James Auter, Theodore Frye, Joshua Robbin Bennett.

B.B./K.W.M.

TWENTY THREE

Charles J. Carter

My Contribution: I was a member of the Brotherly Love Lodge No. 896 of the Grand United Order of Odd Fellows and Chairman of the Committee of Arrangements for Harrisburg's Fiftheenth Amendment Celebration. I was very active in attending Black conventions along with Cassius M. Brown, Sr. and O.L.C. Hughes. I was also the pastor of Free Baptist Church in Harrisburg and organized union camp meetings in Harrisburg for local clergy.

My Legacy: I was an emblem of political engagement in Harrisburg in the fight for equal rights, Republican clubs, and in temperance circles. As a clergyman, I sought to ensure that individuals of color were memorialized well in Harrisburg. Second Baptist Church, where I often spoke and served, still remains today. The decoration of veterans' graves, of which I took part, remains a tradition in Harrisburg and beyond.

About Me: "The orator, Rev. C.J. Carter, delivered an able address, and read a beautiful poem composed by himself for the occasion. It was an affecting and patriotic tribute to the brave soldiers we revere..." — *Harrisburg Telegraph*, May 31, 1873.

Full Name: Charles J. Carter • Birth Date: Ca. 1826 • Death Date: December 21, 1881. Buried in Reading, Pennsylvania. • Place of Birth: Reading, Pennsylvania • Sex: Male • Race: Black • Places of Residence: Reading, Pennsylvania; 49 N. Duke Street (1863), South & River Alley (1867), 1318 William Street (1876-1880), and Marion Street in Harrisburg, Pennsylvania (1870s); Providence, Rhode Island (1874). • Connection to the Old Eighth Ward: Interacted with key players and organizations • Family Members: Wife: Barbara Carter. Daughter: Annie E. Carter (executor of estate). • Education: Unknown • Occupations: Teacher. Clergyman. • Church Membership: Free Baptist Church and Second Baptist Church. • Activism: Grand United Order of Odd Fellows; Brotherly Love Lodge No. 896; Temperance Convention; Hartranft Club; Union Central Republican Club; and Dauphin County Equal Rights Club. • Connections: William Howard Day, Thomas Morris Chester, John Quincy Adams, John W. Simpson, George Galbraith, David Chester, Jacob Costley, William R. Dorsey, Benjamin Foote, Cassius M. Brown, and O.L.C. Hughes.

C.B.

TWENTY FOUR
David R. Chester

My Contribution: I co-founded the Brotherly Love Lodge, Grand United Order of Odd Fellows in Harrisburg. I was so politically influential that I even ran as an independent candidate for Harrisburg Mayor in 1872. In Philadelphia, I was the first person of color elected to the Common Council. I also played for the Harrisburg Monrovian baseball team in 1867 against the Philadelphia Pythians (whose roster included Octavius Catto).

My Legacy: I continued my parents' legacy as a successful restaurateur and activist in Harrisburg before moving to Philadelphia, where I made a significant impact on local politics.

My work in co-founding the Brotherly Love Lodge continues to have relevance, as the Odd Fellows' benevolent and socially engaged work leaves its mark on Harrisburg in a number of ways. My role as a political pioneer—a man of color who ran for and was elected to offices traditionally reserved for white men—continues to hold significance in a society where political roles are still assumed, primarily, by white men.

About Me: "While here he was quite prominent among colored men, being one of the founders of Brotherly Love Lodge, G. U. O. O. F., and attached to other secret orders.... On removing to Philadelphia, Mr. Chester was given charge of one of the public school buildings as custodian, and his influence was such that he was nominated for Common Council and elected by a large majority. He was the only colored man ever elected to this position in Philadelphia." — *Harrisburg Telegraph*, December 11, 1889.

29

Full Name: David R. Chester • Birth Date: August 11, 1835 • Death Date: December 10, 1889. Buried next to wife, Amelia Chester, in Lincoln Park Cemetery in Penbrook, Pennsylvania. • Place of Birth: Harrisburg, Pennsylvania • Sex: Male • Race: Black (1850 and 1880 Federal Censuses) • Places of Residence: 305 Chestnut Street, Harrisburg, Pennsylvania (before 1879); 1041 Lombard Street, Philadelphia, Pennsylvania (1879-1889). • Connection to the Old Eighth Ward: Resided near Eighth Ward; contributed to organizations and churches in the ward including the Odd Fellows Lodge. • Family Members: Father: George Chester. Mother: Jane Chester. Siblings: Thomas Morris Chester, Eliza Chester Zedricks, and Harriet Chester Copley. Wife:

Amelia L. Chester White. • Education: Unknown. • Occupations: Restaurateur (Harrisburg). School Custodian (Philadelphia). Common Council member (Philadelphia). • Church Membership: Unknown—likely Wesley Union A.M.E. Zion Church. • Activism: Brotherly Love Lodge No. 896, Grand United Order of Odd Fellows; Tuesday Night Club (Philadelphia); Old Reliable Club of Pennsylvania (Philadelphia). • Connections: Thomas Morris Chester, Jane Chester, Amelia Chester, William H. Marshall, George Galbraith, and Eliza Chester Zedricks.

H.C.

TWENTY FIVE
Amelia Chester White

My Contribution: I fundraised for the fledgling church that would become Capital Presbyterian Church. I remained active in Harrisburg society circles even after relocating to Philadelphia with my husband.

My Legacy: I invested in my community, making churches for African Americans of Harrisburg fiscally possible. Capital Presbyterian Church, still in existence today, would not be possible without my work.

About Me: "The ladies of the Second Presbyterian congregation of this city, for several months in a sewing circle capacity, have been preparing articles for their annual fair. The cost of erecting a house for worship and purchasing the ground upon which it stands, reaches nearly $4,000.... The ladies hope to be successful enough to pay the portion of the pastor's salary yet due, the interest on church debt, and considerable on the principal.... Mrs. Amelia L. Chester and Mrs. Priscilla Cann have been appointed receivers." — *Harrisburg Telegraph*, February 7, 1873.

Full Name: Amelia Lydia Chester; Amelia Chester White • Birth Date: ca. 1836-1841 (based on estimates from census records and obituary) • Death Date: January 1, 1921. Buried next to her husband, David Chester, in Lincoln Park Cemetery in Penbrook, Pennsylvania. • Place of Birth: Philadelphia, Pennsylvania (1880 *Federal Census*); Columbia, Pennsylvania; or Michigan (1920 *Federal Census*). • Sex: Female • Race: Black (1880 and 1920 Federal Censuses) • Places of Residence: 305 Chestnut Street, Harrisburg, Pennsylvania; 1039 Lombard Street, Philadelphia, Pennsylvania (1880); 49 Greenwood Avenue, Montclair, New Jersey (1920-1921). • Connection to the Old Eighth Ward: Lived a few blocks south of the Eighth Ward. • Family Members: Husband: M1: David R. Chester. Husband: M2: Jacob C. White (married May 12, 1898). • Education: Could read and write. • Occupations: Seamstress. • Church Membership: Elder Street Presbyterian and Capital Presbyterian Church. • Activism: Elder Street Presbyterian Benefit Bazaar Committee; Second Presbyterian Benefit Fair Committee; Miriam Household of Ruth. • Connections: James Auter, David R. Chester, T. Morris Chester, Jane Chester, Annie E. Amos, Josephine Bibb.

K.W.M.

White and Black women stand outside doorways and peer out windows on Tanner's Alley between Walnut Street and Cranberry Avenue. This street was central to the Underground Railroad and a major residential area in the Black community of the Eighth Ward between 1850 and 1913. Jane Chester lived two blocks southeast. Photo ca. 1913 from Record Group 17, Series #17.522, courtesy of Pennsylvania Historical and Museum Commission, Pennsylvania State Archives, Harrisburg, PA.

TWENTY SIX
Jane M. Chester

My Contribution: Along with my husband, I contributed to the abolitionist cause through connections to *The Liberator* and the Underground Railroad. I catered numerous weddings, funerals, socials, and other events for all of Harrisburg, white and black. I owned my own home, where I raised children with great success, took on boarders, hosted events, and made my own taffy.

My Legacy: I escaped enslavement in Baltimore and made a treacherous journey north to Harrisburg, Pennsylvania, where I met the man I married, George Chester, and collaborated with him in the work of operating a restaurant and combatting slavery. After George's death in 1859, I developed a formidable reputation of my own in Harrisburg. The home I owned on Chestnut Street served as a gathering place for the city's organizations, churches, and changemakers, and my catering business served white and black, young and old, and policymaker and commoner. The Capital Presbyterian Church is still in existence, thanks to my support of the Elder Street Presbyterian Mite Society shortly after an 1890 fire destroyed the church building. My husband and I passed our passion for abolitionism on to our son, Thomas Morris Chester, who had a significant impact on African American history in our nation.

About Me: "No colored woman a resident of Harrisburg was better known or more highly respected than Mrs. Chester.... Her life was useful and creditable and she devoted herself to her children for whose good she made many sacrifices. Always pious, charitable and neighbourly, Mrs. Chester was never without devoted friends, and by those who survive her, death will be sincerely mourned." — *The Harrisburg Daily Independent*, March 19, 1894.

Full Name: Jane Maria (Morris) Chester • Birth Date: 1800-1805 (approximate, most likely 1801) • Death Date: April 20, 1894 • Place of Birth: Baltimore, Maryland • Sex: Female • Race: "Colored" (1840, 1850, and 1860 Federal Censuses); Black (1870 and 1880 Federal Censuses) • Places of Residence: Gay Street, Baltimore, Maryland (while enslaved); 305 Chestnut Street, Harrisburg, Pennsylvania. • Connection to the Old Eighth Ward: Resident on Chestnut Street two blocks southeast of the Eighth Ward. Operated restaurant, the State Capitol Hotel, in Eighth Ward; belonged to Wesley Union A.M.E. Zion Church, connected with Elder Street Presbyterian Church. •

Family Members: Husband: George Chester. Children: Charlotte Chester, Thomas Morris Chester, David Chester, Harriett Chester, Maria(h) Chester, Amelia Chester, Eliza Chester Zedericks. (Note: the Chesters had several other children who did not live to adulthood.) • Education: No education listed on federal census records. • Occupations: Restaurateur. Caterer. Homemaker. Boarding House Operator. • Church Membership: Wesley Union A.M.E. Zion Church (member) and Elder Street Presbyterian Church (supporter). • Activism: Involved with the distribution of *The Liberator* and likely the operation of the Underground Railroad; hosted the Mite Society for Elder Street Presbyterian Church. • Connections: T. Morris Chester (son), David Chester (son), Amelia Chester (daughter-in-law), Eliza Chester Zedericks, Anne E. Amos (Mite Society), and James Auter.

K.W.M.

TWENTY SEVEN
Maude B. Coleman

My Contribution: I was an activist and politician who devoted my life to securing democracy for all people. I was a founding member of the Phyllis Wheatley Colored Branch of the YWCA in November of 1919, before its formal organization in 1920. Appointed as Pennsylvania's first Interracial Consultant by Governor Pinchot, I worked with many labor industries throughout Pennsylvania to ensure the employment and safe working environment for African Americans. My successful intervention in racial clashes in Pennsylvania led to similar work in Detroit and Lansing, Michigan. In 1947, I wrote *The History of the Negro in Pennsylvania*, published by the Department of Welfare.

My Legacy: I advocated for the rights of women of color and committed my life to the activist work of interracial reconciliation that still continues today. I was honored by the Francis Harper Club in Harrisburg in 1926. Several organizations named their groups with my name including the Maude Coleman council, the Maude B. Coleman Republican Women of Montgomery County Council, and a community center in Easton, Pennsylvania.

About Me: "Maude Coleman is a woman thoroughly equipped along political lines, having engaged in political, social service, and Y.W.C.A work..." — *Harrisburg Telegraph*, 1920.

Full Name: Maude B. (Deering) Coleman • Birth Date: ca. 1879 • Death Date: February 25, 1953 • Place of Birth: Sparrowsville, Virginia • Sex: Female • Race: "Mulatto" (1910 and 1920 Federal Censuses), "Negro" (1930 and 1940 Federal Censuses) • Places of Residence: Harrisburg, Pennsylvania: 129 Short Street (before 1912) and 641 Boas Street (1920-1953) • Connection to the Old Eighth Ward: Resident at 129 Short Street; advocated for residents of the Eighth Ward threatened by the second Capitol Complex Extension Project; petitioned Governor Duff in 1950 to protect the established African-American neighborhood near Forster Street. • Family Members: Husband: John W. Coleman (Feb 25, 1865-Feb 28, 1948), m. September 3, 1897. Child: Priscilla Coleman, died in infancy. • Education: Graduate of University of Washington, Oberlin College, and Pennsylvania School of Social Work. • Occupations: Special Inter-Racial Consultant for the State Welfare Department for thirty years. Founding member of the Phyllis Wheatley Colored Harrisburg Branch of the YWCA in 1920. First African American tax collector in the country, according to a Pittsburgh Courier article in 1926. Sole "female delinquent tax collector" in Pennsylvania (*Chicago De-*

fender, 1935). • Church Membership: Married at First Baptist Church in Harrisburg; honored with "Maude B. Coleman Day" at Bethel A.M.E. Church in 1926; husband John Coleman was member of Capital Presbyterian Church; Superintendent of Sunday school at Capital Presbyterian; funeral service held at Wesley Union A.M.E. Zion Church with Rev. Garrett Lee (Capital Presbyterian) and Rev. B.T. Glasco (Berean Presbyterian, Philadelphia) officiating. Buried at William Howard Day Cemetery alongside husband. • Activism: Dauphin County Republican Women's Organization (executive board); Dauphin County Organizer of Colored Women; member of Republican City Committee, American Red Cross, Seattle Red Cross Auxiliary, and the Rebecca Aldridge Civic Club of Harrisburg; guest speaker in Harrisburg schools during "National Negro History Week" in 1940; president of the Auxiliary to Harrisburg's branch of the NAACP; State Organizer of Colored Women by the State Committee of Pennsylvania (Republican appointee); State Federation of Colored Women's Clubs (district vice president); Pennsylvania Association of Colored Women (state treasurer and vice president); Pennsylvania State Organization of Social Workers (member, teacher); member of Women's National Republican Organization and the Negro Women's Republican League; Bethune-Cookman College in Florida (advisory board); and Colored Women's Eastern Division of the Republican Party (director). • Connections: James M. Auter, Jr. (co-worker); A. Dennee Bibb and Dorothy Curtis (nearby neighbors); A. Dennee Bibb (fellow Republican); Ida and Cassius Brown, Jr. (YWCA collaborators); Charles Crampton (census committee, NAAC); A. Dennee Bibb (NAACP); and John P. Scott.

M.J.

TWENTY EIGHT
Turner Cooper

My Contribution: I served as dean of the board of elders at Capital Presbyterian Church for decades. I started the Springdale neighborhood in Allison Hill. And I advocated for my son to be able to attend a white school in 1871.

My Legacy: I provided crucial leadership in Harrisburg, in leading Capital Presbyterian Church and pioneering residency in Springdale. Capital Presbyterian Church still stands as a visible marker of my investments during my lifetime.

About Me: "He was one of the early residents of Allison Hill, having moved to that community forty years ago. He was a member of the Capital Street Presbyterian Church for nearly sixty years, serving as dean of the board of elders. He was the oldest member of the Sunday School." — *Harrisburg Telegraph*, February 18, 1929.

Full Name: Turner Cooper • Birth Date: August 2, 1860 • Death Date: February 17, 1929 • Place of Birth: Winchester, Virginia; born enslaved. • Sex: Male • Race: Black • Places of Residence: Harrisburg, Pennsylvania: 133 Walnut Street, 1604 Elm Street, and 1610 Elm Street • Connection to the Old Eighth Ward: Resident on Walnut Street two blocks west of the Eighth Ward; member of Capital Presbyterian Church. • Family Members: Father: Turner Cooper. Mother: Sarah Shepherd Cooper. Wife: Mary Cooper. Children: Porter Cooper, Charles Cooper, Harry Cooper, Ross Cooper, William Cooper, Sarah Cooper, Mary Cooper, and Jennie Cooper. • Education: Could read and write according to federal census records. • Occupations: Butler. Carpenter. Brickyard Worker. Janitor. • Church Membership: Capital Street Presbyterian Church (dean of board of elders and oldest member of Sunday school) • Activism: Unknown • Connections: Jacob T. Compton, Cassius M. Brown, Levi Weaver, and George H. Imes.

TWENTY NINE

Joseph Costley

My Contribution: I was a veteran of the Civil War from 1864-1865, a well-regarded local musician at community and organizational gatherings, and an assessor of the Eighth Ward. I lead the Excelsior Cornet Band.

My Legacy: I synthesized musical talents, political passion, and a spirit of community engagement in order to serve Harrisburg as an agent of change in the North after the Civil War. My work as a community-engaged, politically-active musician served as a precursor to the work of future generations of African American musicians, who used their work to support community change and activism.

About Me: "The Excelsior Cornet Band furnished some very fine music last evening at the display of fireworks at the corner of Third and Walnut streets." — *Harrisburg Telegraph*, July 5, 1871.

Full Name: Joseph Costley. Alternate last name: Castley. • Birth Date: ca. 1842-1843 • Death Date: March 22, 1897. Buried in Philadelphia. • Place of Birth: Pennsylvania • Sex: Male • Race: "Mulatto" (1870 *Federal Census*) and Black (1880 *Federal Census*) • Places of Residence: 605 South Avenue (1869-1882) and 307 Blackberry Avenue (1870-1876) in Harrisburg, Pennsylvania. 845 Ontario Street, Philadelphia, Pennsylvania (1897) • Connection to the Old Eighth Ward: Resident on South Avenue; assessor of ward; performed in Excelsior Cornet Band at numerous events. • Family Members: Wife: Julia Moore Costley. Daughter: Sarah C. "Sallie" Costley. • Education: Trained as a musician. • Occupations: Served in the Civil War from 1864-1865 in Company D of the 32nd Colored Troops Division. Carpenter. Musician. • Church Membership: Unknown • Activism: Excelsior Cornet Band (director); Grand United Order of Odd Fellows, Chosen Friends Lodge. • Connections: William Howard Day, David Stevens, William R. Dorsey, William Battis, John W. Simpson, George H. Imes, and John Q. Adams.

K.H./K.W.M.

THIRTY

Dr. Charles H. Crampton

My Contribution: I was a leading Black voice in Harrisburg in the first half of the twentieth century and the principal African American leader of the Republican party. I served as deputy secretary of the State Health Department and the chairman of the board of managers of the Forster Street YMCA. I wrote a history of Black physicians in Pennsylvania. I was an athletic trainer who helped the athletes at William Penn and a well-regarded public speaker who even led pep rallies before football games. I contributed to many educational organizations and events for people of color.

My Legacy: I consistently used my resources to develop the institutions of Harrisburg's African American community. I advocated for voting rights, brought influential speakers to the city, and helped people whenever I could. As a person of color with a medical degree, I inspired future generations. I also worked against racial segregation in the city. I was a main character in Jackson Taylor's historical fiction work *The Blue Orchard*.

About Me: "Short addresses were given by 11 men, all connected with sports at either old Tech high or at William Penn High. All praised Dr. Crampton's fine work." — *The Evening News*, June 13, 1934.

Full Name: Charles Hoyt Crampton • Birth Date: March 1, 1879 • Death Date: November 15, 1955 • Place of Birth: Harrisburg, Pennsylvania • Sex: Male • Race: "Negro" (Draft Card) and "Mulatto" (1920 *Federal Census*) • Places of Residence: Harrisburg, Pennsylvania: 213 River Avenue, 214 Pine Street, 509 Fourth Street, and 600 Forster Street. • Connection to the Old Eighth Ward: Resident; physician for neighborhood; organized community activities; established Forster Street Branch of the YMCA in nearby Seventh Ward. • Family Members: Father: Benjamin Crampton. Mother: Susan Dorsey. Reared by Col. Frederick Lucious Copeland. • Education: Old Central High School, 1899 (only Black orator in class). Medical Degree from Howard University. Doctor of Humane Letters at Lincoln University, 1944. • Occupations: Physician. Athletic Physician for nearly forty years at two schools: Harrisburg Tech (1917-1926) and William Penn High School (1926-1955). • Church Membership: Capital Street Presbyterian Church (member and chairman). • Activism: Worked or spoke at Republican rallies; headed Black division of the Republican Party in Pennsylvania and served as Vice Chairman in Dauphin County; contributed to Colored YMCA; spoke at colleges in Gettysburg and Pittsburgh; educated African-American women in first aid; held Red Cross rallies; conducted "Peoples Forum" at various churches for twenty years; sued Victoria theatre over segregation in 1913 and won. • Connections: Maude Coleman, C. Sylvester Jackson, Robert Nelson, Aubrey Robinson, and others.

M.E.

THIRTY ONE
Dorothy M. Curtis

My Contribution: I was a prominent soprano in Harrisburg's music community and a dedicated elementary school teacher at Wickersham Elementary School.

My Legacy: I was a talented classical musician and a respected educator in Harrisburg and beyond who selflessly contributed musical talents to local organizations and churches. Second Baptist Church, where I often performed, still operates as an active church community today.

About Me: "She was an often sought-after vocalist. She enjoyed religious and classical music." — Betty Curtis, niece of Dorothy, written history.

Full Name: Dorothy Margarete Curtis; Dorothy (Curtis) Nichols • Birth Date: ca. 1900-1903 • Death Date: January 23, 1955 • Place of Birth: Harrisburg, Pennsylvania • Sex: Female • Race: Black (1910 and 1920 Federal Censuses) and "Negro" (1930 *Federal Census*) • Places of Residence: Harrisburg, Pennsylvania: 127 Short Street, 250 Liberty Street, and 133 Balm Street. • Connection to the Old Eighth Ward: Resident on Short Street. • Family Members: Father: Robert Curtis. Mother: Jane Greenly Curtis. Brothers: John Curtis, Robert Curtis, Earl Curtis, Floyd Curtis, and Orvin Curtis. Husband: Sheridan H. Nichols (m. Jan. 2, 1938). • Education: Cherry State Teachers College (source: interview with descendant Betty Curtis); Shippensburg State Teachers College; University of Pennsylvania summer course; and Temple University summer session. • Occupations: Soloist. Elementary School Teacher at Wickersham School, Harrisburg. Clerk. • Church Membership: Bethel A.M.E. Church. • Activism: Community Choral Society; Alpha Music Study Club (Harrisburg branch of National Association of Negro Musicians); Crispus Atticks Club. • Connections: Mildred Mercer Cannon. Rosabelle Quann. Frisby C. Battis and Maude Coleman (neighbors).

S.R./K.W.M.

THIRTY TWO
J. Steward Davis

My Contribution: I was the first African American to graduate as valedictorian from Dickinson Law School. I became a well-known attorney and trial lawyer who fought for Black rights in Harrisburg, Baltimore, and elsewhere.

My Legacy: I was an ambassador for people of color in law, politics, and advocacy work in Harrisburg, the mid-Atlantic, and the United States as a whole. I fought for Black rights in capital murder cases. And I was a pioneer for Black Democratic activism.

In My Words: "The law offers a most attractive (spot) for colored men. We get a fair show in the courts and the people appreciate our efforts" —*Afro-American Newspaper*, March 11, 1921.

"It is time that we look after our own political affairs, and not entrust them to whites who are indifferent to our welfare" —*Afro-American Newspaper*, July 29, 1921.

Full Name: James Steward Davis • Birth Date: October 11, 1890 • Death Date: Disappeared in 1929 • Place of Birth: Harrisburg, Pennsylvania • Sex: Male • Race: Black (1920 *Federal Census*) • Places of Residence: 418 South Street, Harrisburg, Pennsylvania; 1400 Jefferson Street and 1202 Madison Avenue, Baltimore, Maryland. • Connection to the Old Eighth Ward: Resident • Family Members: Wife: Blanche Moore Davis. Children: Suzanne and Blanche Davis. • Education: Harrisburg High School graduate. Dickinson College, 1916 (first in class). • Occupations: Lawyer • Church Membership: Wesley Union A.M.E. Zion Church (Sunday school assistant superintendent). • Activism: The Bar Association of Baltimore City. • Connections: Matilda Stuart (grandmother).

N.K. **41**

THIRTY THREE
William R. Dorsey

My Contribution: I was the constable of the Eighth Ward and Seventh Ward and an active agent in criminal justice issues and politics within the community of Harrisburg. I served as secretary during the mayoral elections of Harrisburg.

My Legacy: I was a significant leader in Harrisburg's political circles, whether by organizing the Central Blaine Club or Union Republican Central Club, pursuing justice as constable, or organizing meetings in conjunction with the local churches. My political and activist work as a leader in Harrisburg's Black community continues to remain relevant today.

About Me: "Pursuant to a call, the colored citizens of the city met in large numbers on Wednesday evening in the M.E. church in Short street, for the purpose of organizing a campaign club. The meeting was called to order by Wm. R. Dorsey" — *Harrisburg Telegraph*, July 5, 1872.

Full Name: William R. Dorsey • Birth Date: 1834 • Death Date: December 5, 1901 • Place of Birth: Maryland • Sex: Male • Race: Black (1880 *Federal Census*) • Places of Residence: 505 South Avenue, Harrisburg, Pennsylvania. • Connection to the Old Eighth Ward: Resident; constable in Eighth Ward; organizer of political meetings in ward. • Family Members: Wife: Rebecca Washington Dorsey. • Education: Could read and write. • Occupations: Constable • Church Membership: Wesley Union A.M.E. Zion Church. • Activism: Central Blaine Club, President; Union Republican Central Club of Harrisburg Committee; Central Union Club (marshal); and Good Samaritans and Daughters of Samaritan Club. • Connections: William Battis (fellow Republican nominee for various positions in the Eighth Ward) and Joseph P. Popel (Union Republican Central Club).

Ad.L.

THIRTY FOUR
Alice Dunbar-Nelson

My Contribution: I advocated for women's suffrage, war aid efforts, and positive interracial relations in Harrisburg, Pittsburgh, and communities across the Commonwealth of Pennsylvania. My major edited work, *Masterpieces of Negro Eloquence*, published in Harrisburg in 1914, features fifty-one of the best and most famous speeches of Black men and men of America, Africa, and Europe from the nineteenthth and early twentiethth centuries.

My Legacy: I used my talents for writing and speaking and served as an advocate for women's suffrage, war aid, and anti-lynching efforts. I am considered a Harlem Renaissance poet, and my plays, poetry, short stories, and journalism make me an iconic African American writer.

About Me: "I recall, as a kid in Harrisburg, PA, the sweeping grace with which she swept into the large parlor of the Justin Carters before she took the vow which tied her into marital fetters to her present husband, Athletic Commissioner Robert J. Nelson. A Lady-in-Waiting, fresh from the pompous corridors of some 18th-Century French drawing room, was the impression." — Orrin C. Evans, "On a Personal Note," *Afro-American*, April 29, 1933.

"Mrs. Alice Dunbar Wilson, one of the most widely-known colored lecturers and writers in the country today has been secured to speak before the Forum in Wesley Church, Forster street, to-morrow afternoon. Mrs. Wilson is widely-known as a lecturer of note.... The subject of her talk to-morrow 'His Country' is one of interest to all." — *Harrisburg Telegraph*, February 23, 1918.

43

Full Name: Alice Ruth Moore; Alice Dunbar-Nelson. • Birth Date: July 19, 1875 • Death Date: September 18, 1935 • Place of Birth: New Orleans, Louisiana • Sex: Female • Race: Black (1900 and 1920 Federal Censuses), "Mulatto" (1910 *Federal Census*), and "Negro" (1930 *Federal Census*) • Places of Residence: 56 Palmyra Street, New Orleans, Louisiana; Brooklyn, New York (1897-1898); 2236 Sixth Street, Washington, D.C.;1008 French Street, 916 French Street (1909-1923), and 1310 French Street (1926-1932) in Wilmington, Delaware; Philadelphia, PA (1933-1935). • Connection to the Old Eighth Ward: Frequently lectured at Wesley Union A.M.E. Zion Church; husband, Robert, was activist within the Eighth Ward; diary discusses time in Harrisburg; scrapbook of suffragist work includes articles and artifacts relating to speaking engagements and work throughout Pennsylvania, including Harrisburg. • Family Members: Father: Joseph Moore. Mother: Patricia "Patsy" Wright Moore. Husband: M1: Paul Laurence Dunbar, m. 1898-1902. Husband: M2: Henry Arthur Callis, m. 1910-1913. Husband: M3: Robert Nelson, m.1916-1935. • Education: Straight College (now Dillard University); Columbia University; Cornell University; Pennsylvania School of Industrial Art; and University of Pennsylvania. • Occupations: Teacher. Poet. Playwright. Journalist. Newspaper editor. • Church Membership: Episcopal • Activism: Reconstruction and Readjustment Conference (Howard University); Women's Committee of the Council of National Defense; Delaware Republican Convention (delegate); American Interracial Peace Committee (executive secretary); Pennsylvania State Federation of Negro Women's Clubs; and Delaware Crusaders for the Dyer Anti-Lynching Bill. • Connections: Robert Nelson (husband) and W. Justin Carter.

K.W.M./J.T.C.

THIRTY FIVE
William McDonald Felton

My Contribution: I ran a successful auto garage in Harrisburg and later became a master mechanic for automobiles and airplanes. My mechanical school, located at 44 N. Cameron Street, attracted students from across the country. I taught men how to be chauffeurs and to fix automobiles in the decades that saw the revolution in transportation from horse to automobile.

My Legacy: I was a successful entrepreneur in the auto, flying, and entertainment industries. I had a patent issued for my design of a rug and carpet cleaning machine (*Official Gazette of the United States Patent Office, Volume 434*). A poster dedicated to my contributions and legacy is installed at the State Museum of Pennsylvania, and I am celebrated in several published books about African American entrepreneurs and African Americans in the auto industry.

About Me: "the mechanical wizard of the city..." —*Pittsburgh Courier*, October 27, 1923.

Full Name: William McDonald Felton. Nickname: Mack Felton • Birth Date: December 26, 1874 • Death Date: November 18, 1930 (buried in Lincoln Cemetery, Penbrook, Pennsylvania) • Place of Birth: Georgia • Sex: Male • Race: Black (1905 and 1915 Manhattan Censuses) and "Mulatto" (1920 *Federal Census*) • Places of Residence: Georgia; Manhattan, New York City, New York (1905); 655 Briggs Street (1915), 25 N. 11th Street (1920), and 25 N. Cameron Street (1921-1930) in Harrisburg, Pennsylvania. • Connection to the Old Eighth Ward: Resided near the Eighth Ward on Cameron Street. • Family Members: Brothers: Alonza Felton and Eliga Felton. Wife: Josephine Felton. Son: William M. Felton Jr. • Education: Could read and write according to census records. • Occupations: Long Shoreman. Repairman. Chauffeur. Auto Garage manager. Founder of Automobile and Aeroplane Mechanical School. • Church Membership: Second Baptist Church • Connections: W. Justin Carter.

45

C.D.

A photograph of Hannah Braxton Jones (1852-1928), a remarkable woman who lived through the entire period celebrated in the Commonwealth Memorial. She was one of only twenty-two Black women in Harrisburg who owned their own property at the turn of the twentieth century. She resided on Tanner's Alley near Wesley Union A.M.E. Zion Church and then, after the demolition of the Eighth Ward, on Liberty Street west of the capitol. Photo, late 19th century, courtesy of the family of Marian Cannon Dornell.

THIRTY SIX
Edith Fields Murphy

My Contribution: In the year that American women earned the right to vote, I was one of only 34 women appointed to a group of 200 census enumerators to carry out the federal census in Pennsylvania's Eighteenth Congressional District. I worked to collect information from residents in the first precinct of Harrisburg's Seventh Ward, a well-established African American neighborhood. I later became a teacher in Harrisburg before serving the community of Cleveland, Ohio in the metro housing authority. In my retirement in Oberlin, Ohio, I served First Church and played a role as the first African American in integrating Kendal, a retirement community.

My Legacy: I broke ground in enumerating Harrisburg's population and worked to ensure that my community was fully counted. In my teaching career, I had a positive influence on a generation of middle school children. I lived a full life of 99 years, serving the community of Cleveland, Ohio, through a career in the metropolitan housing authority, and later involving myself in my church in Oberlin.

About Me: "More than 200 persons will assist in taking the next decennial census in Dauphin, Cumberland and Lebanon Counties.... The enumerators as announced all have been approved by the Census Bureau at Washington....The appointments in most cases include one person, either a man or a woman, in each voting precinct of the city and county.... Following are those already named.... Edith A. Fields." — *The Evening News*, December 15, 1919.

"I have never known a more gracious person than Edythe - just a perfect delight to be with." — As remembered by Reverend John Elder, former Pastor of First Church in Oberlin, 2020.

47

Full Name: Edith Adalene Fields; Edith Fields Murphy; Edythe Murphy. • Birth Date: 1901 • Death Date: July 15, 1999 • Place of Birth: Pennsylvania • Sex: Female • Race: Black (1920 *Federal Census*) • Places of Residence: 1194 Christian Street, Harrisburg, Pennsylvania; Cleveland, Ohio; Oberlin, Ohio. • Connection to the Old Eighth Ward: Resided two blocks east of the Eighth Ward near Derry and Market Streets; attended Bethel A.M.E. Church; enumerated former residents of the Eighth Ward in the first precinct of Seventh Ward, which ran from Forster Street to Herr Street. • Family Members: Father: Oscar Fields. Mother: Anne Lucinda (Jackson) Fields.

Sister: Mattie Louise Fields. Husband: Luke Alexander Murphy. Cousin: Conrad Ellis. • Education: Harrisburg Central High School, 1919. Cheyney Training School for Teachers in Cheyney, Pennsylvania, with certification to teach middle school, 1924. • Occupations: Census enumerator and teacher in Harrisburg. Cashier and bookkeeper at Cleveland Metropolitan Housing Authority, Cleveland, Ohio. • Church Membership: Bethel A.M.E. Church, Harrisburg; First Church in Oberlin (United Church of Christ), Oberlin, Ohio. • Activism: Mother was president of the Ladies' Usher Board of Bethel A.M.E. Church and Gluck Auf Club in Harrisburg; participated in First Church Sewing Group, Oberlin, Ohio. • Connections: C. Sylvester Jackson, Walter J. Hooper, H. Edwin Parson, Ephraim Slaughter, and Sylvester Burris.

C.B./S.M./D.P.

THIRTY SEVEN
Benjamin J. Foote

My Contribution: I was a trustee of Wesley Union A.M.E. Zion Church, a leading member of Brotherly Love Lodge Number 896 and Chosen Friends Lodge Number 43, and the first African American policeman in Harrisburg.

My Legacy: I was a faithful servant to my city, whether by managing a local business, sustaining the hotel industry, investing in the future of Wesley Union A.M.E. Zion Church, maintaining justice as a police officer, or supporting the work of Harrisburg's secret societies. My upstanding character made me an excellent ambassador of the moral equality of Harrisburg's Black community. My contributions to Harrisburg as the city's first African American policeman retain great relevance today, given contemporary conversations about complicated relationships between race and justice in the nation. Further, my investments in Wesley Union A.M.E. Zion Church and Harrisburg's local chapters of secret societies are evident in the active work that their members still do today.

About Me: "He was the first colored policeman of this city and earned a fine reputation as an efficient, painstaking officer. For upwards of twenty-six years, Mr. Foote had been a consistent, active member of the South Street Wesley A.M.E. Zion Church and was for many years a trustee of said church. He was a widely known worker in secret society circles..." — *Harrisburg Daily Independent*, May 23, 1901.

Full Name: Benjamin J. Foote • Birth Date: March 16, 1833 • Death Date: May 23, 1901 • Place of Birth: Baltimore, Maryland • Sex: Male • Race: "Mulatto" (1870 *Federal Census*) and Black (1880 and 1900 Federal Censuses) • Places of Residence: Harrisburg, Pennsylvania: N. 4th Street & North Street (1867), 502 South Street (1876-1882), 106 Short Street (1885-unknown), 517 State Street (1886-1887), 127 Cranberry Avenue (1889-1893), 626 Walnut Street (1894-1897), 426 State Street (1899), and 515 E. State Street (1901). • Connection to the Old Eighth Ward: Resident; involved in social and political organizations; member of Wesley Union A.M.E. Zion Church. • Family Members: Wife: Ellen Jefferson Foote (1855-1892). Children: Eloise, Fannie, Henrietta, Susan, Anna, Julia, Alfred, Joseph, and Samuel. • Education: Could read and write. • Occupations: Confectioner. Tobacco and Cigar salesman. Hotel porter. Inspector of Elections, Second Precinct (1875). Policeman. • Church Membership: Wesley Union A.M.E. Zion Church • Activism: Dauphin County Equal Rights Club (marshal); Chosen Friends Lodge; Free and Accepted Masons, Number 43 (steward); Grand Order of United Odd Fellows, Lodge Number 896; and Wesley Union A.M.E. Zion Church (trustee). • Connections: Jacob Compton, T. Morris Chester, William Howard Day, John W. Simpson, Charles J. Carter, Zachariah Johnson, David R. Chester, George Galbraith, Joseph Thomas, Joseph Popel, William H. Marshall, John Quincy Adams, Annie E. Amos, David Stevens, John Gaitor, and John P. Scott.

Am.L.

THIRTY EIGHT
Theodore S. Frye

My Contribution: I founded and owned the Frye Hotel, a hub of activity in the final decade of the life of the Eighth Ward. My public legal dispute to transfer my license and hotel to 4th Street after the Capitol Park Extension made me an icon in the fight for Black rights. As both a football team owner and a singer, I supported the cultural well-being of Harrisburg. I also assisted dozens of citizens of the Seventh Ward in voting in 1931.

My Legacy: After the closure of my hotel, I remained active in my community as a foreman of city street cleaning and as an active Republican political advocate. I served as a precursory emblem of the Civil Rights movement as an advocate for my hotel, which served as a hub for African Americans in segregated Harrisburg, before it was demolished during the Capitol Park Extension Project. My advocacy work on behalf of African Americans also represents the long fight for truly equitable voting rights in the United States.

About Me: (Concerning illiterate and blind voters who needed assistance in the Seventh Ward), "Sixty-five were assisted by one man... Theodore Frye, a foreman of the street cleaners of the city highway department." — *Harrisburg Telegraph*, October 26, 1931.

"Theodore S. Frye, for more than 20 years an employee of the city highway department... was active for many years in Republican politics. Frye... was best known as the owner of the Hotel Frye, located in the old Eighth Ward. His hotel and Joe Ganz 'Goldfield' in Baltimore, were the rendezvous of the Negro traveling public in the late nineties. In 1914 he closed his hotel due to the development of the Capitol Park Extension and entered the employ of the city." — *Harrisburg Telegraph*, May 18, 1937.

51

Full Name: Theodore S. Frye • Birth Date: 1867 • Death Date: May 17, 1937 (buried in Lincoln Cemetery, Penbrook, Pennsylvania). • Place of Birth: Harrisburg, Pennsylvania • Sex: Male • Race: "Mulatto" (1880 and 1920 Federal Censuses), Black (1900 and 1910 Federal Censuses), "Negro" (1930 *Federal Census*), and "Colored" (Certificate of Death) • Places of Residence: Harrisburg, Pennsylvania: 501 State Street (hotel, saloon, and eventual residence), 717 Cowden Street (1900-1909), 1004 N. 7th Street (1920-1923), and 635 Boas Street (1928-1937). • Connection to the Old Eighth Ward:

Resident; hotel owner at 501 E. State Street. • Family Members: Father: George Frye. Mother: Julia Green Frye. Wife: Alice L. Woodyard Frye, m. 1889-1937. Son: Leslie Frye. • Education: Able to read and write according to the federal census. • Occupations: Barber. Hotelkeeper. Undertaker. City street inspector (Boas). Foreman of city street cleaners. • Church Membership: Bethel A.M.E. Church; Capital Street Presbyterian Church (funeral) • Activism: Women's Relief Corps; City Republican Committee (member); Wesley Union A.M.E. Zion Church Benefits; Seventh Ward Voters' League; and Verbeke Street Colored YMCA. • Connections: Jacob Compton, Joshua Robbin Bennett, A. Dennee Bibb, Maude Coleman, Peter Blackwell, Frisby C. Battis, George Galbraith, John W. Simpson, James H.W. Howard, Joseph L. Thomas, Leslie A. Marshall, Clarence Williams, Robert J. Nelson, James H. Auter, Percy Moore, Charles Crampton, Henry E. Parsons, Harry Burrs, William H. Marshall, Colonel Strothers, Daniel Potter, John P. Scott, Morris H. Layton, Sr., W. Justin Carter, and Anne E. Amos.

J.R./K.W.M.

THIRTY NINE
John Gaitor

My Contribution: I was a prominent political figure in the Eighth Ward and was elected second district supervisor of Republican party in 1872. I was a respected founding member of Brotherly Love Lodge No. 896, Grand United Order of Odd Fellows. I was an active participant in community events around equality in the Eighth Ward, including the Fifteenth Amendment Celebration.

My Legacy: I cared deeply about the education of Black children and joined the Harrisburg School Board to help create better educational opportunities in Harrisburg's Eighth Ward. A memorial commemorating me and my wife (Mary A. Gaitor) is located in Lincoln Cemetery. My advocacy for high-quality, equitable education remains relevant in Harrisburg today.

About Me: "John Gaitor, one of the original five founders [of Brotherly Love Lodge No. 896, G.U.O. of O.F.] ...spoke of the great benefits which had been secured, and the progress which had been made, and gave great encouragement to press on in the good work." — *Harrisburg Telegraph*, December 7, 1872.

"John Gaitor is one of the most intelligent and worthy colored men of the city. He is honest, capable and intelligent, and will make a good supervisor." — *Harrisburg Telegraph*, February 14, 1876.

Full Name: John Gaitor • Birth Date: September 7, 1820 • Death Date: March 30, 1901 • Place of Birth: Virginia • Sex: Male • Race: "Mulatto" (1850 and 1860 Federal Censuses) and Black (1880 and 1900 Federal Censuses) • Places of Residence: Harrisburg, Pennsylvania: James and Elder Streets (1869), 435 State (1894), and 414 South Street (1897-1900). • Connection to the Old Eighth Ward: Resident; worked and ran for political office in the Eighth Ward. • Family Members: Father: John Gaitor. Mother: Mrs. Amelia Gaitor. Siblings: Mrs. Sarah Wallace, Mrs. Tamson Fitzgerald, Mrs. Mary Jones, Mrs. Jane Snyder, and Mark Gaitor. Wife: Mary Anna Gaitor (d. January 27, 1900). Children: Richard Gaitor, Joseph Gaitor, Idella Gaitor, and Loretta Viola Gaitor. • Education: Could read and write according to federal censuses. • Occupations: Waiter. Confectioner. Fruit Vendor. Caterer. • Church Membership: Wesley Union A.M.E. Zion Church • Activism: served in numerous organizations: Wesley Union A.M.E. Republicans (vice president), Brotherly Love Lodge No. 896, Grand United Order of Odd Fellows (original founding member), Harrisburg School Board (vice president and chairman), and Union Republican Central Club (member); elected Republican Supervisor of Second District. • Connections: Joseph B. Popel (A.M.E. Republican Committee), John Q. Adams and Cassius Brown (Brotherly Love Lodge No. 896), George Galbraith and George H. Imes (fellow Republican candidates), James H. W. Howard (School Board), and William Howard Day. A.R.

FORTY
George R. Galbraith

My Contribution: I was a well-known resident, census enumerator, and acclaimed Republican politician of the Eighth Ward. I was a leading figure in local baseball, acting as team president for Harrisburg's Apolia team and team secretary and team scorer for Harrisburg's Moravians team.

My Legacy: I wed sports involvement with political activism, serving in leadership roles at political meetings, enumerating for the census, and eventually becoming a Republican delegate for the first precinct of the Eighth Ward. In a world in which those involved in athletics also have political voices, my life continues to have great relevance.

About Me: "A man of powerful build" — *The Harrisburg Patriot*, regarding Galbraith's baseball involvement.

Full Name: George R. Galbraith • Birth Date: September 1848 • Death Date: April 27, 1912 • Place of Birth: Harrisburg, Pennsylvania • Sex: Male • Race: "Mulatto" (1850 *Federal Census*) and Black (1900 *Federal Census*) • Places of Residence: Harrisburg, Pennsylvania: 412 South Street, 402 Filbert Street (1900), and 405 Filbert Street • Connection to the Old Eighth Ward: Resident; political activism; census enumerator. • Family Members: Father: George Galbraith, Sr. Mother: Elizabeth [Eliza] Galbraith. Sisters: Lucretia Galbraith, Prescilla Galbraith. • Education: Educated well enough to perform many roles in city • Occupations: Cemetery Superintendent. Census Enumerator for Eighth Ward (1900). Estate Agent (1900). Team Scorer and Secretary for Harrisburg's Moravians Baseball Club. Team President of Harrisburg's Apolia Baseball Club. Politician. • Church Membership: Wesley Union A.M.E. Zion Church • Activism: Served in many community organizations: Old Reliable Club, Equal Rights Club of Dauphin County (officer), and Black Republicans (organized event in 1873 for commemorating the Fifteenth Amendment and the freeing of enslaved people of the West Indies). • Connections: David Chester, T. Morris Chester, Charles J. Carter, Joseph Costley, William Howard Day, John Gaitor, George H. Imes, James H.W. Howard, Joseph B. Popel, John W. Simpson, and David Stevens.

Al.S.

FORTY ONE

Henry H. Garnet

My Contributions: In Harrisburg and across the nation, I spoke constantly about abolition, suffrage, and Black education. I read the Emancipation Proclamation in Harrisburg in 1868 in commemoration of the important declaration, and I inspired the formation of a Garnet League, which was dedicated to Black education.

My Legacy: I am remembered as a prominent advocacy figure for justice, freedom, and equality for people of color in the United States. The Garnet League that I helped to found was committed to fostering quality educational opportunities for African Americans across the country. I gave the now-famous "Address to the Slaves of the United States of America" speech at the National Convention held in Buffalo, New York, in 1843, which elicited even the attention of Frederick Douglass.

In My Words: "Think of the undying glory that hangs around the ancient name of Africa:—and forget not that you are native-born American citizens, and as such, you are justly entitled to all the rights that are granted to the freest. Think how many tears you have poured out upon the soil which you have cultivated with unrequited toil, and enriched with your blood; and then go to your lordly enslavers, and tell them plainly, that you are determined to be free." — Henry Highland Garnet, "Address to the Slaves of the United States of America," 1843

Full Name: Henry Highland Garnet • Birth Date: December 23, 1815 • Death Date: February 12, 1882 • Place of Birth: Kent County, Maryland; born enslaved. • Sex: Male • Race: Black • Places of Residence: William Spencer's Plantation near Chesterville, Maryland; Whitesboro, New York; Liberia. • Connection to the Old Eighth Ward: Spoke at Wesley Union A.M.E. Zion Church and inspired the start of an extremely active Garnet League in Harrisburg. The Garnet League met in the Brotherly Love Lodge, No. 896, of the Grand United Order of Odd Fellows. • Family Members: Wife: Julia Ward Garnet. Children: Henry S. Garnet, Mary Garnet, James Garnet. • Education: African Free School. Oneida Institute. • Occupations: Worked on ships that went to Cuba as a teen. Minister. Abolitionist. Commissioner of the U.S. for Liberia. • Church Membership: Liberty Street Negro Presbyterian Church in Troy, New York, in 1842; Shiloh Presbyterian Church, New York in 1850. • Activism: Member of the anti-slavery Liberty Party; extremely active in abolitionist work; inspired the formation of Garnet Leagues all over the country, including one in Harrisburg; inspired the start of the Henry Highland Garnet Literary Association in the basement of Capital Presbyterian Church. • Connections: Thomas Morris Chester, Annie E. Amos, and O.L.C. Hughes.

E.S.

FORTY TWO
James W. Grant

My Contribution: I faithfully served and led Harrisburg's Black secret societies, in conjunction with Capital Presbyterian Church, in the late nineteenth and early twentieth centuries. I served as the acclaimed Grand Master of the local Chosen Friends Lodge No. 43 of the Masons, and I co-founded the Masonic Home and Orphanage in Linglestown, Pennsylvania, with John Q. Adams, James Auter, and others. I worked in the community as a messenger for the railroad.

My Legacy: My work at the Great Lodge was highly admired, and my desire to help the poor and elderly folks of color in the county received frequent attention in the local newspapers. As a messenger for the Pennsylvania Railroad Office, I was a trustworthy figure, who was important to communication in Harrisburg. The work of the Prince Hall Masons still continues today in Linglestown, where the home that I co-founded was located. Capital Presbyterian Church remains an active church body to this day.

About Me: "Grand Master James W. Grant's administration was commented upon as one of the best in the history of the grand lodge." — "Colored Masons Return," *Harrisburg Telegraph,* December 15, 1909.

Full Name: James W. Grant • Birth Date: April 25, 1850 • Death Date: September 29, 1914 • Place of Birth: Winchester, Virginia • Sex: Male • Race: "Mulatto" (*1880 Federal Census*) • Places of Residence: Harrisburg, Pennsylvania: 5 S. Front Street (1880), 326 Calder Street (1883-1887), 321 Muench Street (1888), 328 Muench Street (1889-1891), 230 Liberty Street (1893), 228 Liberty Street (1894-1895), 340 Muench Street (1897-1900), 704 N. 7th Street (1902-1907), 130 Balm Street (1908), 1727 N. 7th Street (1909-1911), 128 Balm Street (1913), and 303 S. 14th Street (1914). • Connection to the Old Eighth Ward: Frequently spent time in the Eighth Ward, serving as elder of Capital Street Presbyterian Church, a messenger for the nearby railroad, and a member of local Black secret societies. • Family Members: Wife: Hattie M. St. Claire Grant, m. 1890-1914. Children: James W. Grant, Jr., Mary L. Grant, Howard B. Grant, Joseph L. Grant, Sterling S. Grant, Mabel Grant Williams, Louie J. Grant, and Hattie Grant. • Education: Could read and write according to the federal census; educated well enough to do clerical work and social and political engagement. • Occupations: Coachman. Mail clerk for Freight Office. Messenger for Pennsylvania Railroad. • Church Membership: Capital Presbyterian Church (elder). • Activism: Chosen Friends Lodge No. 43 (Worshipful Grand Master and member). • Connections: John Q Adams, John P. Scott, James M. Auter, Frisby C. Battis, James H.W. Howard, Joseph L. Thomas, William H. Jones, Eliza Zedricks, Morris H. Layton, Ida Brown, George H. Imes, W. Justin Carter, and Cassius M. Brown.

I.G.

FORTY THREE
Harriet Harrison Henry

My Contribution: I was a socially active teacher who worked for the betterment of my students. As an elementary teacher, I was able to shape young people for a brighter future.

My Legacy: I made my community better through educational improvement. I educated numerous children of color in Harrisburg and the southern states at a time when few school opportunities were available to them. In that way, my teaching opened new opportunities for students.

About Me: "Miss Harriett Harrison, a school friend of the bride [Catherine Payne] was maid of honor, wearing a beautiful gown of white crepe de chine with lace and crystal trimmings." — *Harrisburg Telegraph*, November 21, 1912.

Full Name: Harriet L. Harrison; Harriet Henry. Nickname: "Hattie." • Birth Date: July 1885 • Death Date: Unknown; after 1956 • Place of Birth: Pennsylvania • Sex: Female • Race: Black (1900-1920 Federal Censuses) and "Negro" (1930-1940 Federal Censuses) • Places of Residence: 1618 Walnut Street and 5 S. Sixteenth Street, Harrisburg, Pennsylvania; Fredericksburg, Virginia; Maryland; 13 N. 57th Street and 28 N. 57th Street, Philadelphia, Pennsylvania. • Connection to the Old Eighth Ward: Taught children from the Eighth Ward. • Family Members: Father: Ralph Harrison. Mother: Betty Harrison. Siblings: Bessie (Harrison) Johnston Anthony, Edward Harrison. Husband: Howard M. Henry. Brother-in-Law: James Anthony. • Education: Harrisburg High School, 1907; Teacher Training School. • Occupations: Elementary school teacher at Wickersham School in Harrisburg and schools in Maryland and Virginia. • Church Membership: Second Baptist Church. • Activism: Singer at Second Baptist Church; Unity Social Club. • Connections: Catherine Payne and Horace Payne (friends); M.H. Layton, Sr. and Ida Brown (colleagues at Wickersham School); Cassius Brown, Jr.; and A. Leslie Marshall.

S.M.   **57**

FORTY FOUR
Walter J. Hooper

My Contribution: I came to Harrisburg from Philadelphia in 1911 at the request of Joseph L. Thomas to serve the Black community in funerals and services. I founded Hooper Memorial Home, one of the first African American funeral homes in central Pennsylvania. I also served as a charter member of Forster Street YMCA and faithfully served Bethel A.M.E. Church as a trustee.

My Legacy: I assumed a unique role in Harrisburg as the owner of a prominent funeral home that served African Americans. I was not just a successful entrepreneur, but I also actively served Harrisburg as an engaged person of faith and had a particular passion for the Forster Street YMCA. Hooper Memorial Home, Inc. still exists today as one of the most prominent funeral homes in Central Pennsylvania and is supervised by my granddaughter, Angela Ulen.

About Me: "Walter J. Hooper Sr. came to Harrisburg from Philadelphia and was recognized by the local media for being on the cutting edge of human preservation and bringing the most advanced embalming techniques with him." — "The Hooper Legacy" (Hooper Funeral Home)

Full Name: Walter Jacob Bertram Hooper • Birth Date: August 11, 1886 • Death Date: July 15, 1939 • Place of Birth: Philadelphia, Pennsylvania • Sex: Male • Race: "Mulatto" (1920 *Federal Census*) and "Negro" (1930 *Federal Census*) • Places of Residence: 604 Forster Street, Harrisburg, Pennsylvania. • Connection to the Old Eighth Ward: Resided near Eighth Ward at 604 Forster Street; served numerous residents by providing funeral services; first African American funeral home at 604 Forster Street, the area of the city where many Eighth Warders migrated after their displacement. • Family Members: Father: Thomas A. Hooper. Mother: Eleanora Lee Hooper. Wife: Alice Price Hooper. Children: Eleanor Hooper, Millicent Hooper, and Walter Hooper, Jr. • Education: Temple University; Echels College of Embalming; trained as an assistant for an elite undertaker in Philadelphia for four years. • Occupations: Funeral director. Undertaker operator. • Church Membership: Bethel A.M.E. Church (trustee). • Activism: Charter member of Forster Street YMCA; charter member of Capital City Undertakers Association. • Connections: Connected to dozens of individuals listed among the 100 Voices; served as undertaker for a majority of the funerals of the individuals; and hosted the funerals of some of these individuals in his funeral parlor.

I.G.

FORTY FIVE
Layton L. Howard

My Contribution: I played a major role in the improvement of Harrisburg's green landscape as well as the city's Black community. I served as a forester for the City Park Department. My father and I published a directory in Harrisburg in 1910 featuring Black businesses and prominent citizens in Pennsylvania. I served my country by registering for military service for World War I in September 1918.

My Legacy: The book that I wrote with my father in 1910, *Pennsylvania Negro Business Directory,* still exists in physical and digital form and remains a valuable historical source for information about and images of the state's Black community of the early twentieth century.

About Me: "Mr. Howard, a graduate of the Technical High School of Harrisburg, is employed by the Park Commissioner of the city and is prominent in forestry and in shrubbery."
— "Howard-Blalock Bridal Yesterday Afternoon," *Harrisburg Telegraph*, June 22, 1918.

Full Name: Layton Leroy Howard • Birth Date: January 20, 1886 • Death Date: October 13, 1918 (died of influenza after a brief honeymoon in Cuba with his wife, Janie). • Place of Birth: Harrisburg, Pennsylvania • Sex: Male • Race: Black (1910 *Federal Census*) • Places of Residence: 306 S. 15th Street and 1013 S. 21st Street, Harrisburg, Pennsylvania. • Connection to the Old Eighth Ward: Knew numerous individuals who lived, worked, and thrived in the Eighth Ward, spotlighting them in the *Pennsylvania Negro Business Directory.* • Family Members: Father: James H. W. Howard. Mother: Ella D. Howard. Wife: Jane Grace Blalock, m. June 21-October 13, 1918. Brother-in-Law: Rev. M. L. Blalock. • Education: Technical High School graduate, 1908 • Occupations: Forester and Tree Surgeon. Allison Hill Laundry (1902-1909). Publisher (co-published with father directory of Black schools, businesses, and men and women in Pennsylvania). • Church Membership: Funeral conducted by pastor at St. Augustine's Episcopal Church; father-in-law, Reverend Blalock, worked at Wesley Union A.M.E. Zion Church. • Activism: Unknown • Connections: James H. W. Howard, Jane Blalock-Charleston, and Esther Popel Shaw.

59

J.S.

An image of a page (88) from the *Pennsylvania Negro Business Directory Illustrated 1910* shows prominent Black state employees in Harrisburg in 1910. Four of the six are among the 100 Voices: James M. Auter (top right), Robert J. Nelson (middle right), Roscoe C. Astwood (bottom left), and Harry Burrs (bottom right). The Negro Business Directory was published by James H. W. Howard and his son Layton Howard in 1910 and remains a wonderful primary source for learning about Pennsylvania Black communities in the early twentieth century.

FORTY SIX
James H. W. Howard

My Contribution: I was active in literary, social, and Democratic political circles in Harrisburg. In addition to serving as councilman for the Eighth Ward and clerking in different offices in the Harrisburg capitol, I published and authored books, journals, magazines, and directories—most notably, *The Pennsylvania Negro Business Directory* in 1910.

My Legacy: My work in publishing, government, and politics left a legacy for my son, Layton Howard, who was a member of Jas. H.W. Howard & Son Publishing Company. My political and literary work lived on long after my work was done through my published works. My numerous associations with other agents of change in the Eighth Ward is noteworthy. As a publisher and writer, my work, *The Pennsylvania Negro Business Directory*, remains an invaluable primary record of distinguished African Americans in Pennsylvania in the early twentiethth century.

About Me: "Mr. Howard is a man of ability and intelligence who has espoused the democratic cause for the reason that he believes the contention of the democracy for tariff reform is founded in justice and equity and that a tariff for monopoly must work injustice to all who labor, be the color of their skin white or black." — *The Patriot*, October 17, 1889.

"Mr. Howard is a man of ability, a forcible writer and has had considerable editorial experience." — *The Patriot*, July 10, 1889.

Full Name: James H. W. Howard • Birth Date: 1856/1862 (estimates based on federal census records from 1880-1910) . • Death Date: Unknown. Howard last listed as living in Maryland in the 1930 census. Last recorded appearance in 1932. • Place of Birth: Ontario, Canada • Sex: Male • Race: "Mulatto" (1880 *Federal Census*) • Places of Residence: 1118 Montgomery Street, Philadelphia, Pennsylvania (1893); 306 S. 15th Street, Harrisburg, Pennsylvania (1900-1910) • Connection to the Old Eighth Ward: Knew the community of the Eighth Ward as his book, *The Pennsylvania Negro Business Directory*, features many of its residents; served as a city councilman for the Eighth Ward. • Family Members: Wife: Ella Dorem (m.1884). Son: Layton Leroy. • Education: Buffalo High School, New York (1875); Sinico Academy (1879). • Occupations: Dealer. Merchant. Member of Marshall & Howard fruit and produce firm.

Publisher of *Howard's Negro American Magazine,* the *State Journal, Howard's Negro American Monthly* (1880-1890), *Pennsylvania Negro Business Directory* (1910), and *The New Era* (1915). City council member, Harrisburg (1885-1888). Writer: *Bond and Free* published in 1886, a novel written with accounts from friends and family of slavery experiences in Virginia, and *Color Struggles* published in 1899. Clerk in the Secretary of State Office (1893-1895), and the Office of State Treasurer (1906-1908). Grand Deputy Marshal. • Church Membership: Mite Society of Elder Street Presbyterian Church (elected officer); Capital Street Presbyterian Church (member); and Bethel A.M.E Church (participated in events). • Activism: Democratic leader, in favor of tariff reform and supporter of Grover Cleveland's presidential candidacy; served on executive committee of Negro Democratic State League of Pennsylvania (1888); spoke at meeting of The Colored Cleveland Reform Club in 1888; chaired Colored Democratic State League (1890); participated in the Colored Men's Protective League: "an organization of colored men, of this city, the object of which is to advance the interest of all colored men—socially, politically and industrially" (*Patrio*t, Sep 5, 1891); elected representative of League to the Afro-American League convention in 1891; served on the Executive Committee of Tariff Reform Club; endorsed by the Cleveland Tariff Reform Club for his name to be placed on the ticket to run for house of representatives for Harrisburg in 1892; nominated to run for City Assessor in Harrisburg in 1893; spoke at a meeting of the city's Tammany Association in support of mayoral candidate Eby and the Democratic cause in 1893; served on the committee to organize the memorial service for Frederick Douglass at Elder Street Presbyterian in 1895; ran on ballot for school director of the Second Ward in 1896; applied to be United States consul to Haiti in 1896; acted as business manager of a musical and literary club held at the office of Joseph L. Thomas in 1905; spoked at a meeting of the Sixth Ward Social Club in 1906; served on the committee for the benefit of Harrisburg Hospital in 1907; gave address at People's Forum at Bethel A.M.E. Church in 1907; assisted with the "50th Anniversary of the Emancipation Celebration and Exhibition," September 15 to October 1, 1913; spoke in an event series put on by the local branch of the NAACP in 1928; spoke at the meeting of National Democratic Negro Voters' League in Washington D.C. in 1932; served as member of Negro Press Association and Negro Business League. Mason (1915). • Connections: William Battis, George Galbraith, John P. Scott, J. Q. Adams, and W. H. Jones, Joseph L. Thomas, William Howard Day, Josephine Bibb, George H. Imes, Daniel Potter, James Grant, Dr. W. H. Jones, W. Justin Carter, Dr. W. H. Jones, Dr. Charles Crampton, Robert Nelson, Joseph L. Thomas, and James Auter, Harry Burrs, Rev. W. Marshall, C.W. Strothers, Luther Newman, Charles Crampton, A. Dennee Bibb, Maude B. Coleman, and W. Justin Carter.

An.S.

FORTY SEVEN
O. L. C. Hughes

My Contribution: I was invested in the important work of the Colored Conventions, ensuring that African Americans had the right to vote and to run for office. I edited *The Progress of Liberty*, a newspaper that advocated for political equality among African Americans (*The Patriot*, 1869). I was an active national voice for African American suffrage and equal education in the state Equal Rights League.

My Legacy: In editing *The Progress of Liberty*, I provided information and guidance for African Americans of their political rights and agency. I served a crucial role in conversations related to African American suffrage and equal educational opportunities. Through this work, I was able to fight for equal justice and advocate for the ratification of the Fifteenth Amendment. My work related to equitable educational opportunities still holds relevance in today's society.

About Me: Mr. Hughes congratulated the Colored Convention "upon the recent victory at the ballot box for law and order and the rights of humanity." — *Harrisburg Telegraph*, November 14, 1868.

"Mr. O. L. C. Hughes then delivered an excellent address on 'The Elevation of the Colored Race, and the means to be used in gaining this laudable end.'" — On O. L. C. Hughes' involvement in the 1869 Colored Convention in Pittsburgh, *Pittsburgh Daily Commercial*, December 29, 1869.

Full Name: Orra L. C. Hughes • Birth Date: October 14, 1836 • Death Date: February 2, 1901 • Place of Birth: York County, Pennsylvania • Sex: Male • Race: Black (1900 *Federal Census*) • Places of Residence: Tennessee (1867); 234 N. Third Street, Harrisburg, Pennsylvania (1867-1871); and 310 South Barry Street, Olean City, New York (1900). • Connection to the Old Eighth Ward: Collaborated with men and women of the Eighth Ward through the state's Colored Conventions after the Civil War. • Family Members: Wife: Mary D. "Maude" Molson Hughes (d. 1881); Daughter: Lulu M. Brown. Son-in-Law: Charles Brown. • Education: Unknown • Occupations: Farm Laborer. Lawyer. Editor and proprietor of the weekly Harrisburg newspaper, *Progress of Liberty*. Teacher. Professor. Superintendent of Colored Schools. Lawyer. • Church Membership: Capital Presbyterian Church (Sunday school leader) • Activism: Served on the Garnet League; Negro National Convention; Fifteenth Amendment Celebration (chair); Pennsylvania Colored Conventions of 1868 and 1869 (speaker, secretary, and president); Pennsylvania State Equal Rights League; and Lancaster County Temperance Union Society. • Connections: William Howard Day, Maude D. Molson Hughes, David R. Chester, Charles J. Carter, Joseph Popel, Zachariah Johnson, Cassius Brown, John Gaitor, George H. Imes, John Q. Adams, and William Strothers.

L.S.

Photograph of a teacher and pupil at the school on North Street near 5th Street in the Eighth Ward. The building was known as the Lincoln School but renamed the William Howard Day School shortly before its demolition in the early 1900s. Several of the educators of the 100 Voices -- Ida Brown Colley, Spencer P. Irvin, Morris H. Layton, Sr., John W. Simpson, James Stuart, and Annie M. Summers had a direct connection. Photo ca. 1913 from Record Group 17, Series #17.522, courtesy of Pennsylvania Historical and Museum Commission, Pennsylvania State Archives, Harrisburg, PA.

FORTY EIGHT

George H. Imes

My Contribution: I fought for the freedom of enslaved Americans in the Civil War. After the war, as an orator and delegate of the Republican party, I fought tirelessly for the freedoms, equality, and opportunities of Black Pennsylvanians. Understanding the critical need for a strong education, I served as a public school teacher, principal, Sunday school teacher, and school board member in the communities of Harrisburg and Steelton. I even at one point ran as the Republican candidate for the Lieutenant Governor position in 1886. I edited local newspapers that championed the fundamental political rights and equality of African Americans.

My Legacy: I advocated for better schools for people of color in Harrisburg and worked to foster new opportunities for their education and economic opportunity in Pennsylvania. I campaigned and spoke constantly for Black political rights as a member of the Pennsylvania State Equal Rights League and the Republican party. I had a major impact on the reform of local education and municipal government through my newspapers and numerous speaking engagements.

About Me: "He enlisted in March 1864, when in his 20th year, leaving home at night with the plan in his mind" —Benjamin Albert Imes on his brother George H. Imes enlisting in the United States Colored Troops in the Civil War (Source: Mary Braxton, descendant)

"He is a man of marked intellectual force, and has always taken a prominent part in the progress of his race." — *Harrisburg Telegraph*, August 24, 1892,

"George H. Imes, of Steelton, one of the most popular colored men in this state, at one time independent candidate for lieutenant governor, one of the originators of the colored state fairs." — *The Gazette*, August 26, 1892.

Full Name: George Hezekiah Imes • Birth Date: October 8, 1844 • Death Date: August 25, 1892 • Place of Birth: Franklin County, Pennsylvania • Sex: Male • Race: "Mulatto" (1880 *Federal Census*) • Places of Residence: 945 Fifteenth Street, Harrisburg, Pennsylvania; Steelton, Pennsylvania • Connection to the Old Eighth Ward:

Taught at schools on South Street and North Street; attended Capital Presbyterian at the northern boundary of Eighth Ward; worked with many men and women who lived in the Eighth Ward. • Family Members: Father: Samuel Imes. Wife: Sadie Imes. Children: Aura Imes, Otho Imes, Amy Imes, Jessie Imes, George Lake. Mother-in-Law: Mary Clarke. • Education: Good education that prepared him for occupation as teacher, principal, and editor. • Occupations: School Teacher and principal at North Street School, Calder Street School, and Cherry Alley School House. Professor. Sergeant in the 43rd USCT, Company D, Infantry (March 11, 1864-October 20, 1865). Editor of the Harrisburg Times and Steelton Press. • Church Membership: Capital Presbyterian Church (joined in 1871), Lost Creek Presbyterian Church in McAlisterville, PA (Source: Mary Braxton, descendant). • Activism: Served as member in civic and political organizations including: the Pennsylvania State Equal Rights League, the Masonic Order, Odd Fellows, Union of Sabbath School Workers, and State Afro-American League; directed Steelton Literary Society; selected as Republican delegate for Harrisburg's Seventh Ward and ran as candidate for Lieutenant Governor; organized as Commissioner for State Fair for Colored People. • Connections: John Q. Adams, James Auter, Josephine L. Bibb, Peter Blackwell, Cassius Brown, William Howard Day, William R. Dorsey, H. H. Garnet, James H. W. Howard, Spencer P. Irvin, Robert J. Nelson, Hamilton Newman, Joseph B. Popel, and Joseph L. Thomas.

M.B.*/A.M./K.W.M.

FORTY NINE

Spencer P. Irvin

My Contribution: I taught and prepared the first African American students for admittance to the high school in Harrisburg. I was the principal of North Street School, which became the Lincoln School, later renamed William Howard Day School, the school of many Eighth Ward residents.

My Legacy: I left a rich legacy through my students, including John P. Scott and William H. Marshall. The John P. Scott Elementary School still operates in Harrisburg today in honor of one of my most distinguished students. I was politically engaged as an abolitionist and served alongside William Howard Day in the People's League. I also left a legacy through my son, Spencer P. Irvin, Jr., an esteemed medical doctor at Mercy Hospital in Philadelphia.

About Me: "The first supervisory principal of the schools in this building was Spencer P. Irvin, a teacher of great ability. He it was who prepared the first colored pupils for the High school. Amongst the number were two prominent citizens of today, Prof. John P. Scott and Rev. William H. Marshall. So thoroughly did he do this work that their examination was one of the most brilliant ever recorded in Harrisburg of grammar schools pupils applying for admission to the High School. Mr. Irvin was determined to leave no loop-hole for invidious comparison in regard to the first colored scholars who would be brought in direct scholastic competition with the white students of the city." — *Harrisburg Patriot*, 1913, J. Howard Wert.

Full Name: Spencer Potter Irvin • Birth Date: April 14, 1855 • Death Date: July 3, 1932 • Place of Birth: Philadelphia, Pennsylvania • Sex: Male • Race: Black (1900 *Federal Census*), "Mulatto" (1910 *Federal Census*), "Negro" (1930 *Federal Census*), and "Colored" (Certificate of Death) • Places of Residence: 414 South Street and 406 Cowden Street, Harrisburg, Pennsylvania; 1157 S. 19th Street, Philadelphia. • Connection to the Old Eighth Ward: Resident; teacher and principal at North Street School; member of People's League alongside William Howard Day. • Family Members: Father: Charles Irvin (Haiti). Mother: Caroline Potter (Philadelphia). Wife: M1: Ida Jones. Wife: M2: Anna Louisa Jones Irvin. Son: Spencer P. Irvin, Jr. • Education: Served as teacher and principal in Harrisburg schools. • Occupations: Teacher and principal at Lincoln School. • Church Membership: Unknown • Activism: served in People's League • Connections: George H. Imes, William H. Marshall, and John P. Scott.

C.D.

Photograph of Bethel A.M.E. Church on State Street and West Avenue, a stone's throw away from the State Capitol. The church was one of two African Methodist Episcopal churches in the Eighth Ward. At least nineteen of the one hundred voices had some connection to this church. Photo ca. 1913 from Record Group 17, Series #17.522, courtesy of Pennsylvania Historical and Museum Commission, Pennsylvania State Archives, Harrisburg, PA.

FIFTY

C. Sylvester Jackson

My Contribution: I worked for the advancement of Harrisburg's Black community. As grand trustee of the Elks Lodge for over 25 years, I led and raised funds for Forster Street YMCA, and served as president of the Harrisburg chapter of the NAACP and treasurer for Harrisburg Housing Authority. I was especially concerned with fair housing for the city's African American population.

My Legacy: I was an active member of local fraternal organizations and an advocate for the equality of the Black community. Later in my life, I became a leading advocate for fair housing and today a section of public housing in Harrisburg named after me.

About Me: "The annual meeting of the Harrisburg branch of the National Association for the Advancement of Colored People was held last night in the Bethel A.M.E. Church. C. Sylvester Jackson was elected president of the association...The association was founded with the purpose of promoting closer fellowship between the races and the Harrisburg branch has both white and colored persons as members." — *The Evening News*, December 13, 1918

Full Name: Charles Sylvester Jackson • Birth Date: August 6, 1883 (Draft Registration Cards) or 1884 (Federal Census Records) • Death Date: December 13, 1963 • Place of Birth: Harrisburg, Pennsylvania • Sex: Male • Race: Black (1910 *Federal Census*), Black/"Colored" (1920 *Federal Census*), "Negro" (1930 and 1940 Federal Censuses), "Colored" (1963 Death Certificate) • Places of Residence: Harrisburg, Pennsylvania: 214 N. River Street (1907), 21 N. 15th Street, and 434 Boas Street (1940-1963). • Connection to the Old Eighth Ward: Many close friends and collaborators; involved in Bethel A.M.E. Church. • Family Members: Father: Charles Jackson. Mother: Mary Nelson Jackson. Brother: Robert Jackson. Wife: Violet C. Williams Jackson, m. July 19, 1905-December 13, 1963. Niece: Minnie Williams. • Education: Harrisburg High School graduate, 1903. • Occupations: Stenographer (1910). Private Secretary for John Boyd Estate (1917-1940). Secretary (1963 - death certificate). • Church Membership: Bethel A.M.E. (superintendent). • Activism: Actively involved in community organizations, political organizations, and church: Forster Street Colored YMCA (member drive leader and boys' Bible class leader); State Executive Committee for YMCA (member); Pennsylvania Elks Unity Lodge No. 71 (grand trustee); NAACP Harrisburg chapter (president 1919); Harrisburg Housing Authority (treasurer); song festival at Bethel A.M.E. Church (master of ceremonies); and C. Sylvester Jackson Boys' Bible Class of the YMCA. • Connections: James Auter, Alexander Dennee Bibb, Cassius M. Brown, Sylvester E. Burris, Harry Burrs, W. Arthur Carter, W. Justin Carter, Dr. Charles Crampton, Walter Hooper, Leonard C. Johnson, Dr. William E. Marshall, Robert J. Nelson, Dr. Henry Edwin Parsons, and Daniel Potter.

I.G.

FIFTY ONE
Zachariah Johnson

My Contribution: I was a prominent local minister, music teacher, and property owner in the Eighth Ward who was very active in ensuring political rights in my community. I worked diligently for the equality of Black citizens after the Civil War both on a local level as the president of the Equal Rights Club of Dauphin County, and as a participant in national conventions. I led programs to commemorate the passing of the Fifteenth Amendment and marched as marshal in a parade celebrating U.S. Colored Troops buried in Harrisburg.

My Legacy: I served a crucial role as a music teacher and person of color in Harrisburg who was also engaged in community efforts related to suffrage, equity, and memorialization of African American veterans. My work as a music teacher and activist can still be seen in ongoing celebrations of the Fifteenth Amendment ratification, including the project that has inspired this set of biographies.

About Me: "Zachariah Jonson was the first Negro music teacher of this area." — *The Evening News*, January 22, 1949.

Full Name: Zachariah Johnson • Birth Date: January 1820 • Death Date: after June 1900 • Place of Birth: Maryland • Sex: Male • Race: "Mulatto" (1870 *Federal Census*) and Black (1880 and 1900 Federal Censuses) • Places of Residence: 428 South Street, Harrisburg (owned from ca. 1867-1900). • Connection to the Old Eighth Ward: Resident and property owner on South Street. • Family Members: Wife: Ellen E. Scott Johnson, m. April 5, 1855. Children: William B. Johnson, Leonard Z. Johnson. • Education: Could read and write according to the federal census. • Occupations: Whitewasher. Laborer. Preacher. Minister. Musician. Music Teacher. • Church Membership: Bethel A.M.E. Zion Church. • Activism: Involved in organizations promoting political rights of African Americans: Negro National Convention; Equal Rights Club of Dauphin County (president); Fifteenth Amendment Celebration parade (aid); and Decoration Day Committee. • Connections: Leonard Z. Johnson, O.L.C. Hughes, Joseph B. Popel, David R. Chester, Cassius M. Brown, T. Morris Chester, William Howard Day, William R. Dorsey, George Galbraith, Charles J. Carter, John Q. Adams, Benjamin Foote, and Matilda Stewart (neighbor).

I.S./K.W.M.

FIFTY TWO
Leonard Z. Johnson

My Contribution: I was one of Harrisburg's and Steelton's foremost Black educators and a Presbyterian minister. I was a prominent English professor at Howard University.

My Legacy: I impacted Harrisburg, Princeton, Baltimore, and Washington, D.C., as a teacher, clergyman, and professor with a relentless commitment to high-quality education. I was a leader in the creation of the Steelton Hygienic School, and my advocacy efforts within Black education still remain relevant today.

About Me: "Dr. Leonard Z. Johnson, Sr., one of the first Negro educators of this area." — *The Evening News*, January 22, 1949.

Full Name: Leonard Z. Johnson • Birth Date: June 17, 1870 • Death Date: January 15, 1949 • Place of Birth: Harrisburg, Pennsylvania • Sex: Male • Race: "Mulatto" (1870, 1880, and 1910 Federal Censuses), Black (1900 and 1920 Federal Censuses), and "Negro" (1930 and 1940 Federal Censuses). • Places of Residence: 428 South Street, Harrisburg, Pennsylvania (1880 and 1900); 1615 Druid Hill Avenue, Baltimore, Maryland (1910); Washington D.C.: 918 Westminster Street NW (1920-1930), 1236 Howard Street NW (1935-1949). • Connection to the Old Eighth Ward: Resident until at least age 30. • Family Members: Father: Zachariah Johnson. Mother: Ellen Johnson. Brother: William Johnson. Wife: Louise A. Peebles Johnson, m. October 18, 1904-1942. Children: Louise K. Johnson, Leonard Z. Johnson, Jr., Ellen P. Johnson. • Education: Harrisburg Boys' High School, 1887 (graduated with honors, delivered graduation oration); Lincoln University, Bachelor's degree; Princeton University, Master's degree, 1904 (oration delivered by Woodrow Wilson, then college president); Lincoln University, Doctor of Divinity, 1906. • Occupations: Teacher in Harrisburg and Steelton. Clergyman for Presbyterian churches in Baltimore and Princeton. English Professor, Howard University, 1920-1949. • Church Membership: Presbyterian. • Activism: The Douglass Association. • Connections: Zachariah Johnson (father), Henry Highland Summers.

I.G.

FIFTY THREE

Dr. William M. Jones

My Contribution: I forcibly resisted the Fugitive Slave Act and actively partnered with others in Harrisburg to secure freedoms for escaping enslaved people. I made Harrisburg my home and used my knowledge of Wilkes-Barre, my hometown, to benefit those I assisted as I moved escapees northward.

My Legacy: Hardworking and determined, I dedicated my life to the improvement of conditions for people of my race. Brought together through shared causes, the activism network that I participated in had a long reaching impact on many.

About Me: "'Pap Jones' was a large, well-built man.... For many years, Mr. Jones was one of the most efficient men connected with the 'Underground Railroad' in this locality. He had acquired a thorough knowledge of the routes leading northward and was always prepared to furnish competent guides. His large covered wagon drawn by two horses and driven by himself in the capacity of rag merchant was frequently to be met with on the roads leading towards Wilkes-Barre or Pottsville." — *Harrisburg Telegraph*, January 29, 1887.

Full Name: William M. Jones. Nickname: "Pap" • Birth Date: 1791 (*Harrisburg Telegraph*, August 3, 1881) or 1793 • Death Date: August 1, 1881 • Place of Birth: Kingston, Luzerne County, Pennsylvania • Sex: Male • Race: Black (1870 *Federal Census*) • Places of Residence: Wilkes Barre, Pennsylvania. Harrisburg: 422 South Street, 432 South Street. • Connection to the Old Eighth Ward: Resident. Dedicated church member of Wesley Union A.M.E. Zion Church. Partnered with others in the neighborhood to create a network of allies and secure safe passage on the Underground Railroad. • Family Members: Wife: Mary Jones. Children: Mary Jones, Henry Jones, David Jones, Margaret Jones, Charles Jones, Juliann Jones, Mrs. William Steward. • Education: Trained as a druggist with Mr. Calendar and Dr. D.W. Gross (*Harrisburg Telegraph*, August 3, 1881). • Occupations: Pharmacist. Medical Doctor. Laborer/molder in a foundry. Preacher and organizer. • Church Membership: Wesley Union A.M.E. Zion Church. • Activism: Wesley Union A.M.E. Church (deacon); social activist and organizer of benevolent societies for the African American community; founded Black cemetery (*Harrisburg Daily Independent*, March 31, 1883). • Connections: Fellow activists and transporters in the Underground Railroad: Harriet McClintock Marshall, Joseph Cassey Bustill, Jane Chester, and Mary Bennett.

72

S.M.

FIFTY FOUR

Hannah Braxton Jones

My Contribution: I was a music teacher, church founder, and activist in the Eighth Ward. I fought for temperance and the right of women to vote. I was also one of the few Black women who owned property in the city in the early twentieth century.

My Legacy: I helped to found Second Baptist Church in 1869, which still operates to this day. The home I owned in Harrisburg would be worth nearly $68,000 today.

About Me: "Led by the Spirit of God, a few faithful soldiers of Christ saw a field for labor in this city, and in the year of our Lord eighteen hundred and sixty-nine, the Second Baptist Church had its beginning ....with the following persons: Joseph Braxton (father of Hannah)...and Hannah Braxton..." — *Second Baptist Church Mortgage Burning Ceremonies Program,* 1944.

Full Name: Hannah Braxton; Hannah Braxton Jones • Birth Date: May 12, 1852 • Death Date: May 1, 1928 • Place of Birth: Williamsburg, Virginia • Sex: Female • Race: Black (1870, 1900, and 1920 Federal Censuses) and "Mulatto" (1880 and 1910 Federal Censuses) • Places of Residence: Williamsburg, Virginia. Harrisburg: 134 Tanner's Avenue, 232 Liberty Street. • Connection to the Old Eighth Ward: Resident on Tanner's Alley from the time parents brought the family to Harrisburg in 1866 until the Capitol Extension caused its destruction. Taught music there as well. • Family Members: Father: Joseph Braxton (1820-1890). Mother: Charlotte Cole Braxton (died 1868). Siblings: Mrs. Susan Braxton Carrington (wife of Robert); Mrs. Ann Maria Braxton Taylor (wife of Reuben); Joseph Braxton, Jr. Husband: Min. George W. Jones, m. 1873. Children: James Joseph Jones (born 1874), Mary Ann Jones (born 1877), Alfred Braxton (adopted son). Grandchildren: Dr. George A. Jones, MD. of Steelton, Pennsylvania (known for his work in community health) and Mrs. Hannah Scott Cannon, Nurse. Great granddaughter: Mrs. Marian Cannon Dornell, author of a collection of poetry, *Unicorn in Captivity*. • Education: No formal education • Occupations: Music Teacher, Domestic Worker. • Church Membership: Second Baptist Church, Harrisburg, Pennsylvania • Activism: Second Baptist Church (first lady, deaconess, Sabbath School organizer and administrator, choir organist). Club No. 1, Organized in 1879 (president for 48 years until her death in 1928; instrumental in bringing renowned opera singer, Ms. Marian Anderson, to Harrisburg). • Connections: Grandmother of Mrs. Hannah Scott Cannon.

C.S.G.*

FIFTY FIVE

Dr. William H. Jones, Jr.

My Contribution: I was an experienced doctor for residents in my neighborhood. I was an advocate and supporter of public education for African American children. I was also a major player in Harrisburg's City Beautiful Movement, influencing my community to support the vote for civic improvement and beautification projects.

My Legacy: Respected by both African American and white residents of Harrisburg, I was an active and visible figure. After my death, the Black community raised funds to support a park entrance and fountain in my honor at the Twelfth Street Playgrounds. From education to trade to medical societies, I left a lasting impact on the betterment of Harrisburg.

About Me: "His ability was recognized by all, and he was greatly respected, not only by members of his own race, but by the white people of Harrisburg." — *Democratic Messenger*, Snow Hill, Maryland, January 21, 1905.

Full Name: Dr. William Harrison Jones, Jr. • Birth Date: August 10, 1860 • Death Date: January 19, 1905 • Place of Birth: Snowhill, Maryland • Sex: Male • Race: Black • Places of Residence: Snowhill, Maryland; Knoxville, Tennessee; 402 E. State Street, Harrisburg, Pennsylvania (city resident for 16 years). • Connection to the Old Eighth Ward: Resident; advocate of education and beautification; neighborhood doctor. • Family Members: Father: William H. Jones. Mother: Esther A. (Smith) Jones. Siblings: Georgianna Jones Wilson, Milcah Jones Bailey, John David Jones. Fiancee: Margaret W. Lewis. • Education: Howard University (1887). New York Polyclinic Institute. • Occupations: Barber in Snowhill, MD. Physician. Elected School Director (1902-1904). • Church Membership: St. Paul's Protestant Episcopal Church. • Activism: Active in Republican politics, Black organizations, and medical societies: Academy of Medicine in Harrisburg (president); Brotherly Love Lodge, No. 896, Grand United Order of Odd Fellows; American Medical Society; Pennsylvania State Society; Dauphin County Society; and Baker Building and Loan Association (president). • Connections: Harry Burrs and James Auter, William H. Jones, Sr.

S.M.

FIFTY SIX
Agnes Kemp

My Contribution: I was an educated and articulate physician, who spoke up for the freedom of African Americans in Harrisburg and the political and social rights of women. I broke ground as the first woman accepted into the Medical Society of Dauphin County and gained a reputation as a respected physician. I was an active community organizer and a Sunday school teacher, who started the local chapter of the Women's Christian Temperance Union and worked for the underprivileged in society.

My Legacy: I provide an example of someone who's will to serve affected great change. My role in working for change for the Women's Christian Temperance Union in the city went hand in hand with my work as a suffragist and with benevolent causes. I worked alongside and lectured with the likes of Sojourner Truth, Frances Harper, Julia Howe, and William Lloyd Garrison.

About Me: "At a time in the history of this century, when to be recognized as an anti-slavery man or woman was to subject one's self to persecution and often to physical danger, and then to declare one's self in sympathy with equal political and civil rights for women, was to become socially anathematized, it required no small amount of moral courage in the young matron upon her return home, to prove her 'faith by her works.' But she was equal to the demands of the hour. Firing a few souls with her own lofty zeal, and laughing at all her obstacles, she brought successively to Harrisburg these sturdy pioneers of our latter-day glory, and helped them to sow the seed of a higher patriotism in the conservative capital of Pennsylvania." — *Harrisburg Daily Independent*, December 5, 1895.

75

In My Words: "You say a man has inherent rights. Why has a woman no inherent rights? I say if a man has, a woman has... some of us will no longer be imposed upon; we would rather deny ourselves that sweetest of all elements, the bliss of love, than sacrifice a principle." — May 25, 1870.

Full Name: Agnes Kemp • Birth Date: ca. 1823 • Death Date: May 20, 1908 • Place of Birth: Harrisburg, Pennsylvania • Sex: Female • Race: White • Places of Residence: Harrisburg: 207 N. 2nd Street, Liberty Street, and 2nd Street; Philadelphia, Pennsylvania; Zurich, Switzerland; Swarthmore, Pennsylvania. • Connection to the Old Eighth Ward: Worked with the leaders of the Eighth Ward to promote abolitionism and voting rights for women. • Family Members: Father: Anthony Nininger (1816-1868). Mother: Catharine May Nininger (died when Agnes was an infant). Brother: John Nininger. Husband: M1: Colonel William Saunders, died. Husband: M2: Joseph Kemp (1860). Children: Marie Antoinette Kemp, and two children who died in infancy. • Education: Women's Medical College in Philadelphia, 1879; spoke French and German. • Occupations: Physician and Doctor (M.D.). Activist. Writer. Orator. • Church Membership: Market Square Presbyterian Church. • Activism: Dedicated to temperance, virtuous living, and women's suffrage; spoke at the celebration of the passing of the FifteenthAmendment in Harrisburg; gave Wildwood Park to the city of Harrisburg; selected as delegate to Women's National Council in Washington D.C. 1899; abolitionist; founded Magdalene asylums, home for women, and Women's Christian Temperance Union in Harrisburg. • Connections: Francis Harper.

M.E.

FIFTY SEVEN

Morris H. Layton, Jr.

My Contribution: As a doctor in Harrisburg, I helped many citizens with their health, but I was also busy with church and civic affairs. I tirelessly worked to establish the Forster Street YMCA as a place of recreation and health for our youth. I also was active in local fraternal and professional development organizations.

My Legacy: My legacy is the success of the Forster Street YMCA. Also, my work in the tuberculosis clinic aided the public health of the city and local students through awareness and testing, which eventually led to a decline in positive cases.

About Me: "He practiced medicine in Germantown and Carlisle before opening offices in this city and since has served as president of the Forster street YMCA board of directors and as a trustee of the Wesley AME Zion Church." — *Harrisburg Telegraph*, June 5, 1944.

Full Name: Morris H. Layton, Jr. • Birth Date: August 23, 1887 • Death Date: June 4, 1944 • Place of Birth: Harrisburg, Pennsylvania • Sex: Male • Race: "Mulatto" (1910 and 1920 Federal Censuses), "Negro" (1930 and 1940 Federal Censuses) • Places of Residence: 708 East Street (1900-1910) and 930 N. 6th Street (1920-1940), Harrisburg; Philadelphia, Pennsylvania; Germantown, Pennsylvania; Carlisle, Pennsylvania. • Connection to the Old Eighth Ward: Resident; physician and public health advocate; attended church in ward. • Family Members: Maternal grandmother: Harriet Marshall. Maternal grandfather: Eby Marshall. Father: Morris H. Layton, Sr. Mother: Ella Marshall Layton. Siblings: Ira L. Layton, Marshall Layton, Harriet "Hattie" R. Layton. Wife: M1: Daisy (Chapman) Layton (d. 1912). Wife: M2: Olive Nelson Layton. Child: Olive (Layton) Harris. Son-in-Law: Thomas Harris. • Education: Harrisburg High School, 1905 (salutatorian). Philadelphia Medico-Chirurgical College, 1910. • Occupations: Physician • Church Membership: Wesley Union A.M.E. Church • Activism: President of the Forster Street YMCA board of directors (president); Wesley Union A.M.E. Church (trustee); Sanhedrin Court and The Knights of the Round Table; Officer of State Association of Colored Doctors, Dentists and Druggists; Alpha Musical Club, National Association of Negro Musicians (advisor); Dauphin County Medical Society; Tuberculosis Clinic on Sixth Street. • Connections: A. Dennee Bibb, Dr. Charles Crampton, C. Syvester Jackson. Related to Harriet Marshall (grandmother), Rev. W. H. Marshall (uncle), A. Leslie Marshall (cousin), Dr. William E Marshall (cousin), and Morris H. Layton, Sr. (father).

77

S.M.

FIFTY EIGHT

Morris H. Layton, Sr.

My Contribution: I was among the first generation of African Americans to teach in the city school system when I began my career in 1877. I prepared William H. Marshall and John P. Scott to be the first two African Americans to graduate from the high school in Harrisburg in 1883. I worked to create quality educational opportunities for my students and established a school library at Lincoln School. I was also involved in church and political activities in Harrisburg.

My Legacy: I taught and influenced two generations of students over the course of 50 years. My students became leaders in the Harrisburg community. I had four children, including Dr. Morris H. Layton, Jr., who worked for the betterment of their communities.

About Me: "He was the 'finest instructor in colored schools that Harrisburg ever had and his teachings exerted a lasting influence upon his scholars, many of whom are leading and respected Negro citizens of the community today" — Dr. Charles H. Crampton, *The Evening News*, December 12, 1938.

Full Name: Morris Hallowell Layton, Sr. • Birth Date: September 2, 1856 • Death Date: December 11, 1938 • Place of Birth: Burlington County, New Jersey • Sex: Male • Race: Black (1880 and 1900 *Federal Census*), "Mulatto" (1910 *Federal Census*) and "Negro" (1930 *Federal Census*) • Places of Residence: Philadelphia, Pennsylvania: Ward 8, District 22; 805 Locust St; Harrisburg, Pennsylvania: 512 Briggs Street, 708 East Street, and 930 N. 6th Street. • Connection to the Old Eighth Ward: Lived just outside of the ward; teacher of children in ward; involved in Wesley Union A.M.E. Zion Church and other organizations within the ward. • Family Members: Father: Major Layton. Mother: Rebecca (Steven) Layton. Siblings: Mary E. Layton, Anna Layton, Mrs. Warren Jackson, Norbert P. Layton, William H. Layton, Leon Layton, Florence Layton. Wife: M1: Ella (Marshall) Layton, m. 1887, d. 1906. Wife: M2: Margaret (Matthews) Layton, m. 1911. Wife: M3: Letitia B. Layton, m. 1921, divorced 1927. Father-in-Law: Eby Marshall. Mother-in-Law: Harriet Marshall. Children: Morris H. Layton, Jr., Ira L. Layton, Marshall Layton, Harriet "Hattie" R. (Layton) McFadden. Daughter-in-Law: Olive N. Layton. • Education: Institute for the Colored Youth. Cheyney State Teachers College, 1876. • Occupations: Supervisory principal of Lincoln School. Teacher of night school, Lincoln building. Supervisory principal of the William Howard Day building. Teacher of sixth grade. Wickersham building Mail clerk. Grand Union hotel, Saratoga, New York (over 15 summers). • Church Membership: Wesley Union A.M.E. Zion Church. • Activism: Involved in Republican politics. Harrisburg Christian Endeavor Union. • Connections: Rev. W. H. Marshall (brother-in-law), Dr. A. Leslie Marshall (nephew), Dr. William E. Marshall (nephew), Joseph Popel, John W. Simpson, John P. Scott.

S.M.

FIFTY NINE
A. Leslie Marshall

My Contribution: I led a life of service related to civic, cultural, and arts organizations and improvement societies. My advocacy for improved public health awareness and immunizations impacted and protected Harrisburg's vulnerable populations.

My Legacy: My work and support of local organizations led to enriching the lives and health of my neighbors. Many of the organizations for which I volunteered such as the YMCA, Boy Scouts, and Wesley Union A.M.E. Zion Church still have an active presence in Harrisburg and benefit thousands of residents.

About Me: "Well liked, popular, not only among members of his own race, but with those of every creed and color, he was a distinct credit to his race and championed their every cause to the fullest extent of his ability. Doc had no office hours set aside—he just kept on going around the clock." — Nobe Frank, *Harrisburg Telegraph*, February 5, 1942.

Full Name: Alexander Leslie Marshall • Birth Date: January 5, 1889 • Death Date: February 2, 1942 (buried at Lincoln Cemetery) • Place of Birth: Harrisburg, Pennsylvania • Sex: Male • Race: Black (1900 *Federal Census*), "Mulatto" (1920 *Federal Census*) • Places of Residence: Harrisburg, Pennsylvania: 516 Spruce Street, 631 Boas Street, and 825 N. 6thStreet. • Connection to the Old Eighth Ward: Resided just north of the Eighth Ward; local doctor and engaged in many local organizations; attended church at Wesley Union A.M.E. Zion Church. • Family Members: Grandfather: Alexander W. Dennee. Grandmother: Harriet (McClintock) Marshall. Father: William H. Marshall. Mother: Mary Lillian "Bessie" (Dennee) Marshall. Siblings: William Elisha Marshall, Dr. Forrest Scott Marshall, Catherine Condel (adopted sister). Wife: Margaret (Blalock) Marshall, m. July 6, 1916. Children: Margaret Jane (Marshall) Smith, and Mary E. Marshall. • Education: Central High School, Harrisburg, 1905. Medico-Chirurgical College (later merged with University of Pennsylvania), 1910; residency at Mercy Hospital. • Occupations: Physician. • Church Membership: Wesley Union A.M.E. Zion Church. • Activism: Colored Knights of Pythias; Central PA Medical Society (secretary); National Medical Association (vice president); Forster Street YMCA (president); Wesley Union A.M.E. Zion Church (treasurer); Republicans precinct committee, 8th Ward (secretary); Dauphin County Civic and Progressive League (chairman); WPA Folk Council, Festival of Nations (chairman); Auxiliary Disaster Committee of Harrisburg Red Cross; Hall Johnson Negro Choir (officer); Clinic Committee of Tuberculosis and Health Society of Harrisburg; Housing Association of Harrisburg (executive committee); Scoutmaster and founder of colored Boy Scouts in Harrisburg; Cosmopolitan Chorus, Wesley Union A.M.E. Zion Church (advisor);

Junior Colored Baseball League (president); Community Choral Society (chairman); NAACP, Harrisburg chapter (vice president). • Connections: Alexander Dennee Bibb (cousin), William H. Marshall (father), William Elisha Marshall (brother), Harriet (McClintock) Marshall (grandmother), Morris H. Layton, Jr. (cousin), Morris H. Layton, Sr. (uncle), and Josephine Dennee Bibb Davidson.

S.M.

SIXTY
Harriet M. Marshall

My Contribution: I assisted with efforts in the Underground Railroad. Alongside my mother, Catherine McClintock, I clothed, fed, and educated freedom seekers. One of those who escaped slavery, Elisha Marshall, became my husband.

My Legacy: I helped to construct a monument dedicated to African Americans who fought in the Civil War, and that monument still stands in Lincoln Cemetery today. I worshipped and served for decades at Wesley Union A.M.E. Zion Church, the church that remains to this day. My family's multigenerational legacy in Harrisburg continues to resound. I am represented in a mural on the side of Jackson House.

About Me: "She had been a resident of Harrisburg nearly all her life and has been a member of Wesley Union A.M.E. Zion for sixty years." — *Harrisburg Telegraph*, July 25, 1925.

"During the early years of her young womanhood she assisted with the care of the 'Underground Slaves,' in old Wesley Church. This work was taking place in the midst of terrific conflict over slavery. She with others helped to feed, clothe and care for sick and well; then helped to establish or sent the slaves on to another station. She often told of the gratitude of escaped slaves but was always very secretive about the details." — from *The Descendants of Catherine Yellotz William McClintock, Harrisburg, Pennsylvania, 1770's* (family history compiled by descendant Olive Layton Harris, 1977).

Full Name: Harriet McClintock; Harriet McClintock Marshall • Birth Date: August 14, 1840 • Death Date: July 25, 1925 (buried in Lincoln Cemetery, Pennbrook, Pennsylvania) • Place of Birth: Harrisburg, Pennsylvania • Sex: Female • Race: Black (*1900 Federal Census*) and "Mulatto" (*1920 Federal Census*) • Places of Residence: Harrisburg: 175 Paxton Street, 708 East Street, and 930 N. 6th Street. • Connection to the Old Eighth Ward: Resident; life-long member of Wesley Union A.M.E. Zion Church (her mother Catherine helped to found the original church). • Family Members: Mother: Catherine McClintock. Husband: Elisha B., m. June 9, 1864. Children: William Marshall, Elisha Marshall, Ellis Marshall, M. Ella Layton. Son-in-Law: Morris H. Layton, Sr. Grandchildren: Dr. A. L. Marshall, Dr. William E. Marshall, Dr. Forrest S. Marshall, Dr. Morris H. Layton, Jr., Marshall L. Layton, Hattie R. Layton McFadden, Ira L. Layton. • Education: Educated at the German School; could read and write according to the federal census. • Occupations: Teacher. Domestic Servant for the Eby Family on Front Street. • Church Membership: Wesley Union A.M.E. Zion Church. • Activism: Underground Railroad. • Connections: William E. Marshall, Catherine McClintock, William H. Layton, M.H. Layton, Sr., M.H. Layton, Jr., Forrest S. Marshall.

D.G.

SIXTY ONE
William E. Marshall

My Contribution: I provided quality service and advice for Harrisburg's African American community through my pharmacy on Boas Street, which was opened for decades. I also invested in Black sports leagues and brought entertainment acts to the city. I was well-connected.

My Legacy: My pharmacy was long running and was a staple of the Harrisburg community for more than two generations. Segregation notwithstanding, my support and promotion of Black sports teams fostered high-level competition among athletic teams and provided entertainment for the city.

About Me: "If you had a date with one of the girls you always wound up in Bud Marshall's Drug Store having a coke or an ice cream soda, and they had booths in the back. Bud was quite a talker and a kidder and joker and he really had the personality. He had something to say to everybody that came in." — Mr. Robert Quann interview on Black Harrisburg in the 1920's and 1930's, February 27, 1977.

"The druggist, who has been host to many celebrated Negroes... has assisted many a boy with guidance and advice." — *Patriot*, March 11, 1951.

Full Name: William E. Marshall. Nicknames: Doc Marshall, Bud Marshall. • Birth Date: July 5, 1890 (WWI Draft Card), or July 7, 1893 (WWII Draft Card), or July 7, 1890 (Death Certificate) • Death Date: February 25, 1953 (Mechanicsburg, Pennsylvania) • Place of Birth: Harrisburg, Pennsylvania • Sex: Male • Race: Black (1900 *Federal Census*), "Mulatto" (1920 *Federal Census*) • Places of Residence: Harrisburg: 629 Boas Street, 516 N. 5th Street; 230 W. Simpson St, Mechanicsburg, Pennsylvania. • Connection to the Old Eighth Ward: Resident. Opened pharmacy one block north of Eighth Ward; promoted sports events in community including football, basketball, and baseball; attended Wesley Union A.M.E. Zion Church. • Family Members: Grandfather: Alexander Dennee. Grandmother: Harriet Marshall. Father: William H. Marshall. Mother: Mary Lillian "Bessie" (Dennee) Marshall. Siblings: William Elisha Marshall, Dr. Forrest Scott Marshall, Catherine Condel (adopted sister). Wife: Rose K. (Comminger) Marshall. Father-in-Law: John William Comager. Mother-in-Law: Emma Comager. Sisters-in-Law: Edith Comager, Georgia Ann Comager, Mrs. J.W. Craighead. • Education: Harrisburg High School, 1907. Philadelphia College of Pharmacy, 1911. • Occupations: Pharmacist. Negro Baseball team owner and promoter. • Church Membership: Wesley Union A.M.E. Zion Church • Activism: Pennsylvania Medical, Dental, and Pharmaceutical Association; Junior League of Harrisburg Colored Baseball (president); Owner of Harrisburg Governors Football; Harrisburg Homes Company (board); Forster Street YMCA; Harrisburg Scholastics (organizer/manager). • Connections: Dr. A. Leslie Marshall (brother and neighbor on Boas Street), Alexander Dennee Bibb (cousin), William H. Marshall (father), Harriet (McClintock) Marshall (grandmother), Josephine Dennee Bibb Davidson (aunt), Morris H. Layton, Jr. (cousin), Morris H. Layton, Sr. (uncle), Morris H. Layton, Jr (cousin).

S.M.

SIXTY TWO
William H. Marshall

My Contribution: As part of the first African American cohort to graduate high school in Harrisburg, I became a well-known teacher and principal of the Calder School for 29 years, and I even instructed a night school for illiterate adults. I was also a minister who devoted my time and resources to establishing the A.M.E. church in Harrisburg and other Pennsylvania communities.

My Legacy: My devotion to fulfilling and expanding others' hunger for knowledge, either through schooling or religion, improved the lives of so many. Through my leadership, I forged a greater sense of community among Harrisburg's African American population that spawned opportunities for growth and betterment in later generations.

About Me: "Working in all movements for the advancement and uplift of his race, Dr. Marshall spent devoted efforts in all civic affairs in addition to his labors as an educator and a minister." — *Harrisburg Daily Independent*, March 20, 1916.

"No one man of color in central Pennsylvania was so actively identified with all phases of public life and those elements which go to make for racial and community uplift as was Rev. Marshall. His acquaintance was country-wide and the scope of his activities was by no means limited to his own immediate vicinity." — *Harrisburg Newspaper*, March 1916.

Full Name: William Howard Marshall • Birth Date: January 1, 1865 • Death Date: March 18, 1916 • Place of Birth: Harrisburg, Pennsylvania • Sex: Male • Race: "Mulatto" (1870 and 1880 Federal Censuses) and Black (1900 and 1910 Federal Censuses). • Places of Residence: 175 Paxton Street, 516 N. 5th Street, 516 Spruce Street, and 629 Boas Street in Harrisburg, Pennsylvania; Port Deposit, Maryland. • Connection to the Old Eighth Ward: Resident. Significant involvement in Wesley Union A.M.E. Zion Church. • Family Members: Father: Elisha B. Marshall. Mother: Harriet (McClintock) Marshall. Sister: Mariah Ella (Marshall) Layton. Wife: Mary Lillian "Bessie" (Dennee) Marshall. Father-in-Law: Alexander W. Dennee. Mother-in-Law: Francis Dennee. Brother-in-Law: Morris H. Layton, Sr. Sister-in-Law: Josephine Dennee Bibb Davidson. Children: Catherine Condol (adopted daughter), Dr. A. Leslie Marshall, William E. Marshall, Dr. Forrest S. Marshall. Daughters-in-Law: Margaret (Blalock) Marshall, Rose K. (Comminger) Marshall. Grandchildren: Margaret Jane (Marshall) Smith, Mary E. Marshall. • Education: Harrisburg High School, 1883. • Occupations:

Principal of the Calder School. Pastor of the Harris Chapel. Summer Mail Clerk, Grand Union Hotel, Saratoga Springs, New York. • Church Membership: Member of Wesley Union A.M.E. Zion Church. Pastor of Harris Chapel. • Activism: Brotherly Love Lodge, No. 896, Grand United Order of Odd Fellows (building committee, noble father); Grand Lodge of the State of Pennsylvania; Chosen Friends' Lodge, No. 43, Free and Accepted Masons; Dauphin County courts (Probation officer); *Star of Zion*, Charlotte, North Carolina (Contributor); A.M.E. Zion Philadelphia and Baltimore Annual Conference (Secretary). Helped form the Harris Chapel on Marion Street. • Connections: Dr. A. Leslie Marshall (son), William E. Marshall (son), Alexander Dennee Bibb (nephew), Harriet (McClintock) Marshall (mother), Josephine Dennee Bibb Davidson (sister-in-law), Morris H. Layton, Jr. (nephew), and Morris H. Layton, Sr. (brother-in-law).

S.M.

SIXTY THREE
Jessie Matthews Vann

My Contribution: I was a top student in Harrisburg's Central High School and the only African American graduate in the class of 1904. I became an excellent teacher in Harrisburg for a number of years. Following my husband's death in 1940, I held lead roles as president and treasurer of *The Pittsburgh Courier*, the largest African American newspaper in the world with a circulation of 300,000. I was a political advocate locally, regionally, and nationally for Black citizens and women of color.

My Legacy: I used my education to become one of the most prominent figures of my day in the field of journalism and advocated for the rights of African Americans as well as women. *The New Pittsburgh Courier* still stands as a representation of my legacy. I remain a memorialized figure in the historic publication, *The Crisis*.

About Me: "She played a big role in Pittsburgh...in the world of many people. She will be missed grievously." — *Pittsburgh Courier*, June 17, 1967.

"She assumed an active role in the publication of the Pittsburgh Courier.... in 1940. Under her direction, the paper became the largest Negro weekly newspaper in the country." — *Pittsburgh Post Gazette*, June 8, 1967.

Full Name: Jessie E. Matthews; Jessie M. Vann; Mrs. R. L. Vann • Birth Date: 1885 • Death Date: June 7, 1967 • Place of Birth: Flora Dale near Gettysburg, Pennsylvania • Sex: Female • Race: Black (1900 *Federal Census*) • Places of Residence: 313 Nectarine Avenue, Harrisburg, Pennsylvania (1904-1907); 6430 Jackson Street, East Liberty, Pennsylvania (at time of death in 1967). • Connection to the Old Eighth Ward: Attended school with many Eighth Warders; member of community organizations in the ward; and attended church at Bethel A.M.E. Church. • Family Members: Sister: Margaret B. Matthews. Brother-in-Law: Lewis W. Matthews. Husband: Robert Lee Vann. Foster-Daughter: Mrs. Mabel Johnson. • Education: Harrisburg Central High School (1904). • Occupations: Teacher. Publisher/Vice President of *The Pittsburgh Courier*. • Church Membership: Bethel A.M.E. Church; Holy Cross Episcopal Church, Pittsburgh. • Activism: Elliott Association; Capital City Waiters Association (recitation performer); Phyllis Wheatley YWCA; served on board of directors for: Pittsburgh YWCA; Urban League Pittsburgh Chapter; NAACP Pittsburgh Chapter; Hill City Municipality; Pittsburgh Conference of Christians and Jews; Department of Public

Assistance of Allegheny County; and the national women's organization Link, Inc. Member of Virginia Union University; National Newspapers Publishers Association; National Council of Negro Women; and National Association of Colored Women's Clubs. Contributed to the Governor's Committee on Industrial Race Relations and the International Development Advisory Board; delegate to Republican conventions; appointed by President Eisenhower as delegate to inauguration of the President of Liberia; served as Daughters of the King at Holy Cross Episcopal Church. • Connections: Sylvester Burris, A. Dennee Bibb, Luther Newman, Matilda Stewart, Harry Burrs, Rev. William H. Marshall, W. Arthur Carter, Professor Morris H. Layton, Ida Brown, George H. Imes, Dr. William H. Jones, C. Sylvester Jackson, and Joseph L. Thomas.

O.B./K.W.M.

SIXTY FOUR
Catherine McClintock

My Contribution: I lived a full life with a major impact on my church and community through leadership, activism and faith. Born in Highspire, Pennsylvania to Geramn parents, I was one of the founders of Wesley Union A.M.E. Zion Church and assisted numerous men and women pass through the Underground Railroad. I helped to raise funds for a monument to USCT members.

My Legacy: I worked within Wesley Union A.M.E. Zion to make the church a thriving hub. The monument to USCT members who fought valiantly in the Civil War stands today in Lincoln Cemetery as does a state historical marker noting my influence. When I died at age ninety, I left behind 100 relatives who grew into the storied Marshall and Layton families of Harrisburg.

About Me: "Harrisburg lost one of its oldest citizens this morning ... Mrs. McClintock has lived in this city over 80 years, and was conversant with local history. She has for over 70 years been a consistent Christian, and was one of the founders of the South Street A.M.E. Zion Church.... She peacefully fell asleep in Jesus, whom she long had served. Mrs. McClintock was of an unusually cheerful disposition, and her acquaintances in this city are most numerous. By her death the community loses one who in early life did much for this city's development." — *Harriburg Telegraph*, April 18, 1893.

Full Name: Catherine Yellotz Williams; Catherine McClintock. Alternate first name: Catharine. • Birth Date: December 13, 1802/1803 • Death Date: 1893 • Place of Birth: Highspire, Pennsylvania • Sex: Female • Race: "Mulatto" (1850 and 1880 Federal Censuses); White German (family history) • Places of Residence: Harrisburg, Pennsylvania: South Ward (1850-1863), 175 Paxton Street (1863-1888), 708 East Street (1889-1892). • Connection to the Old Eighth Ward: Resident during her later years; active member of Wesley Union A.M.E. Zion Church. • Family Members: Husband: M1: Husband: James Williams. Husband: M2: Henry McClintock. Daughters: Mariah Williams Powell, Elizabeth Williams Kelly, Harriet McClintock Marshall, and Catherine "Kate" McClintock White. • Education: Unknown. • Occupations: Unknown. • Church Membership: German Lutheran Church at 3rd and Chestnut Streets, Wesley Union A.M.E. Zion Church. • Activism: Underground Railroad, Benevolent Society. • Connections: Harriet McClintock Marshall (daughter), William H. Marshall, William E. Marshall, Morris H. Layton, Jane Chester, Elisha Marshall, Benjamin Foote, and James Stocks.

K.H.

Photograph of the other African Methodist Episcopal Church in Harrisburg's Eighth Ward: Wesley Union A.M.E. Zion Church at the corner of Tanner's Alley and South Street, also near the State Capitol. Nearly half of the one hundred voices had some documented connection to this church. Photo ca. 1913 from Record Group 17, Series #17.522, courtesy of Pennsylvania Historical and Museum Commission, Pennsylvania State Archives, Harrisburg, PA.

SIXTY FIVE
Mildred Mercer Cannon

My Contribution: I was a talented musician—a vocalist, organist, and pianist—who performed in churches, public events, and radio programs in Harrisburg and the surrounding communities of central Pennsylvania. I was also a dedicated teacher at the Calder School where I helped many children succeed in life, and I served as a mentor to other teachers. I was especially involved in the Phyllis Wheatley YWCA both as a musician and as a representative of young professional women.

My Legacy: Although I had a difficult life—losing both parents when I was a child—I emerged from these tribulations to bless the African American communities of the region with musical performances, recitals, and service. I also helped to usher in generational change through my commitment to the causes of the organizations of professional women at the YWCA.

About Me: "Miss Mildred Mercer will play the signature song, 'The Negro National Anthem.' Miss Mildred Mercer is in charge of this program."—at an event of the Negro Achievement Broadcast —*The Evening News*, February 13, 1931.

"Miss Dorothy Curtis, lyric soprano, assisted by Miss Mildred Mercer, pianist, will present a program at the A.M.E. Church ... Both Miss Mercer and Miss Curtis are teachers in the public schools of this city." — *The Evening News*, March 29, 1930.

Full Name: Mildred Armithine Mercer; Mildred Mercer Cannon • Birth Date: December 28, 1902 • Death Date: January 10, 1986 (buried in William Howard Day Cemetery, Steelton, Pennsylvania) • Place of Birth: Pittsburgh • Sex: Female • Race: Black (1920 *Federal Census*), "Negro" (1930 *Federal Census*) • Places of Residence: 211 Carroll Street, Pittsburgh; Harrisburg: 150 Balm Street, 129 Balm Street (1920 and 1930), 21 N. 15th Street (after 1933) • Connection to the Eighth Ward: Was child when the Eighth Ward was uprooted; contributed to church communities in and near the Old Eighth, performing on the piano and serving as accompanist to important vocalists for area events. • Family Members: Grandmother: Harriet Hawkins. Father: James Nathan Mercer. Mother: Rachel (Hawkins) Mercer. Brother: James Nathan Mercer. Maternal Aunt: Earo Hawkins White, and her husband James H. White. Husband: Paul Lawrence Cannon, b. 1907 (Virginia), m. 1933-1975. Sister-in-Law:

Hannah Scott Cannon. Children: Paul Cannon, Susan Cannon, Mildred Cannon, and Laura (Cannon) Williams. • Education: Central High School; Froehlich School of Music; Cumberland Valley State Normal School (Shippensburg State Teacher's College), 1923; Columbia University (between 1923 and 1933); Elizabethtown College, certification in special education (mid-1950s) • Occupations: Public School Teacher at the Calder School • Church Membership: Wesley Union A.M.E. Zion Church; Second Baptist Church; Capital Presbyterian Church • Activism: Team captain of anti-fly campaign, public health event in Harrisburg undertaken by the State Auxiliary Junior Health League of Colored Girls and the Division of Public Health Education of the Pennsylvania Department of Health; served on waitress committee for the Welcome Home supper in Harrisburg for returning soldiers from World War I; active musical contributor as vocal accompanist and pianist at events at the Phyllis Wheatley YWCA and regional churches; involved in Professional Women's Club at YWCA (delegate for convention at Cheney School for business girls); and "The Negro Achievement Program" on local radio (assistant director). • Connections: Hannah Scott Cannon (Sister-in-Law), James M. Auter, Rosabelle Quann, A. Dennee Bibb, and Ida Brown.

L.C.W.*

SIXTY SIX
Maud Molson Hughes

My Contribution: I was a lecturer best known for advocating for the vote for African American men and especially women after the Civil War. I spoke widely on the theme of "impartial suffrage"—equal political rights for women and men—at Colored Conventions and Equal Rights Leagues in Pennsylvania and New York.

My Legacy: I was a powerful voice for the political rights of Black women to vote at a time when most people favored only male suffrage. I spoke up for the view that women could succeed in any professional or literary occupation if only given the equality of opportunity.

About Me: "She was introduced to the audience by Prof. O. L. C. Hughes, editor of the *Progress of Liberty*, who, in introducing her, said he did not endorse her views on female suffrage. Miss Molson delivered her lecture in a very pleasing manner, and her subject was handled in such a manner as to evince great care in its preparation. She is outspoken in favor of suffrage for all, and especially for females, who, she thinks, have as great a claim to vote as the men have. She met the objections that are usually advanced against female suffrage, and handled the 'lords of creation' without gloves. Her style of delivery is similar to that of Anna Dickinson, and her elocution, if anything, is more perfect." — *Harrisburg Telegraph*, September 15, 1869.

Full Name: Mary D. Molson; Maud Molson Hughes. Nickname: Maud. • Birth Date: September 26, 1846 • Death Date: August 26, 1881 • Place of Birth: Williamsport, Pennsylvania • Sex: Female • Race: "Mulatto" (1860 *Federal Census*), "Quadroon" (*The Brooklyn Daily Eagle* 1869) • Places of Residence: Addison, New York • Connection to the Old Eighth Ward: Spoke at Wesley Union A.M.E. Zion Church in 1869; participated in the jubilee procession of emancipation in 1869 through the Eighth Ward; knew prominent community members. • Family Members: Father: John Molson. Mother: Louisa Clark Molson. Siblings: James S., Ellen R., John, Samuel J., Josey, and Charles Summer Molson. Husband: Orra L. C. Hughes. Daughter: Lulu Missouri (Hughes) Brown. Grandchildren: David, Flora, Anna, and Wesley Brown. • Education: Alfred University, 1862-1863 (graduated with highest honors). • Occupations: Lecturer and Orator. • Church Membership: Unknown. Lectured at Wesley Union A.M.E. Zion Church. • Activism: Prominent participant in Jubilee celebration of emancipation in Harrisburg (1869); member of National Woman Suffrage Association (NWSA); popular national speaker for the equal rights of African American men and women to vote. • Connections: O. L. C. Hughes (husband), David Stevens, Henry H. Garnet, William R. Dorsey, Edward Bennet, and Laura Robinson.   N.K.

Contrary to some editorials in Harrisburg daily papers, the Eighth Ward was hardly a blight or dirty neighborhood at the time of its demolition. The successful City Beautiful Movement, which the city's Black community overwhelmingly supported, left the neighborhood with paved streets, upgraded buildings, a glimmering capitol, and a half dozen paid street sweepers. Here one of these men sweeps Filbert Street near Walnut. Photo ca. 1913 from Record Group 17, Series #17.522, courtesy of Pennsylvania Historical and Museum Commission, Pennsylvania State Archives, Harrisburg, PA.

SIXTY SEVEN
Percy C. Moore

My Contribution: I faithfully served the residents of Harrisburg's Eighth Ward in its final days as a representative of the city's common council. I supported the unification and organization of Black voters to make their voices heard through the polls and was a supporter of the City Beautiful movement in the city. I spent my life dedicated to the betterment of my community through leadership of local organizations including the Masons and Wesley Union A.M.E. Zion Church.

My Legacy: I worked to change the perception of the Eighth Ward to the outward community and worked with the city to make real changes on behalf of our community, including increased police patrol and beautification. I am remembered through the naming of a masonic lodge, Percy C. Moore Lodge 140 in Philadelphia.

About Me: "Mr. Moore is a gentleman of worth to the community and we are confident that if elected, he will serve the people of his ward acceptably and look out for the interests of the whole city." — *Harrisburg Telegraph*, February 14, 1910.

"Mr. Moore takes an active interest in all race enterprises and is looked upon favorably by the leaders and moulders of public sentiment in Harrisburg." — *Pennsylvania Negro Business Directory 1910.*

Full Name: Percy Clinton Moore • Birth Date: January 25, 1877 • Death Date: February 18, 1947 • Place of Birth: West Virginia • Sex: Male • Race: Black (1920 *Federal Census*), "Negro" (1930 and 1940 Federal Censuses) • Places of Residence: 414 South Street (1911), 522 South Street (1912), 417 Walnut Street (1913), 1220 N. Seventh Street, and 625 Harris Street, Harrisburg, Pennsylvania; Mont Alto Sanatorium. • Connection to the Old Eighth Ward: Lived immediately north in the Seventh Ward; represented Eighth Ward as city council member; member of Wesley Union A.M.E. Zion Church. • Family Members: Father: Richard Moore. Mother: Mary E. (Banks) Moore. Sibling: Reuben Moore. Wife: Cora Alice (Simmons) Moore. Father-in-Law: Landreth Simmons. Sister-in-Law: Lillie Simmons. Children: Charles Moore, Percy Moore, Jr. Granddaughter: Sandra Kay Moore. • Education: Storer College, West Virginia • Occupations: Waiter and caterer. Member, city common council, Eighth Ward (1910-1912). Stenographer, State Fire Marshal Department. Clerk, State Capitol. Bureau of Fire Protection of the Pennsylvania State Police. • Church Membership: Wesley Union A.M.E. Zion Church. • Activism: Chosen Friends Lodge No. 43 (member and Worshipful Grand Master), Wesley Union A.M.E. Zion Church (various offices), Common Councilman, Harrisburg Homes Company (Board of Directors), City Beautiful efforts in Eighth Ward, William C. Sproul Republican League of Dauphin County, Citizens' Club (Founder; club to unite all Black voters of the city), WWI Draft Board. • Connections: William E. Marshall served on the Board of Directors of the Harrisburg Homes Company. Supporter of Republican political efforts with Luther Newman, Harry Burrs, Dr. Charles Crampton, and Dr. A. Leslie Marshall.

S.M.

SIXTY EIGHT
Robert J. Nelson

My Contribution: I was a state worker who led organizations for racial justice and equity in Reading and Harrisburg. I published *The Advocate-Verdict*, an important Black newspaper, and edited other newspapers. I directed of religious education at Capital Street Presbyterian Church. I married Alice Dunbar-Nelson, my partner in equity work.

My Legacy: I was a respected journalistic and political voice in central Pennsylvania and the broader mid-Atlantic. My political work with the NAACP and other similar organizations continues to bear fruit today as these organizations continue to thrive.

About Me: "Robert J. Nelson, of this city, was chosen for a third term as president of the Afro-American Republican League of Pennsylvania... He was given the compliment of a re-election by acclamation. Mr. Nelson is a clerk in the Mining Department at Harrisburg and has a side circle of friends." — *Reading Times*, June 17, 1904.

Full Name: Robert John Nelson • Birth Date: May 20, 1873 • Death Date: February 2, 1949 • Place of Birth: Reading, Pennsylvania • Sex: Male • Race: "Mulatto" (1880 *Federal Census*), Black (1900 and 1910 Federal Censuses), "Negro" (1930 *Federal Census*) • Places of Residence: Reading, Pennsylvania: 1048 Cherry Street, 337 ½ North 11th Street, and 340 N. 11th Street; Harrisburg, Pennsylvania: 147 Balm Street, Walnut Street, 149 Linden Street, and 600 Forster Street; Wilmington, Delaware. • Connection to the Old Eighth Ward: Resident; involved in civic organizations in Eighth Ward; published *Masterpieces of Negro Eloquence* with Alice Dunbar-Nelson at 504 N. 4th Street. • Family Members: Father: Levi Nelson. Mother: Harriet Clark Nelson. Wife: M1: Mary "Elizabeth" Robinson Nelson, m. June 26, 1902 - May 22, 1907. Wife: M2: Alice Ruth Moore Dunbar-Nelson, m. April 20, 1916. Children: Harriet Elizabeth Clark and Robert Clark. • Education: Reading Public Schools. • Occupations: Clerk (Mining Department, Harrisburg). Porter. Messenger. State Athletic Commission member. Editor of *Advocate-Verdict, Wilmington Advocate,* and *Washington Eagle.* Publisher of *Masterpieces of Negro Eloquence.* Real Estate Dealer. Assistant Director of Public Safety (Philadelphia). Acting Fire Marshal (Philadelphia). • Church Membership: Capital Street Presbyterian Church (superintendent of Sunday school). • Activism: Afro-American Republican League of Pennsylvania (president), Colored Professionals and Businessmen (member), Harrisburg NAACP (secretary), Harrisburg People's Forum (president), Colored People for Independence (director - Wilmington), Mohican Club in Harrisburg, Colored Elks (member). Sued Victoria theatre over segregation in 1913 and won. • Connections: Alice Moore Dunbar-Nelson, W. Justin Carter, W. Arthur Carter, Jessie Matthews, James Auter, Cassius M. Brown, and George H. Imes.

97

L.T./K.W.M.

SIXTY NINE
Charlotte Newman

My Contribution: I was an active leader in the Household of Ruth, No. 1, a women's organization that worked alongside the Grand United Order of Odd Fellows. I belonged to the Household of Ruth at a time when discrimination kept Black people out of fraternal orders. I also supported the work of my husband, Hamilton Newman, to extend political rights to people of color in my community.

My Legacy: Through my leadership in the Household of Ruth, I created an organization that fostered charitable work and incredible social and economic good for the African American community in Harrisburg.

About Me: "This Order is also the main living embodiment of the answer to the thirty-year old challenge to us as colored citizens to— "do something." We have accomplished it. We have not simply copied others. We have created the Household of Ruth, the sisterhood of our lodges..." — William Howard Day, *Harrisburg Telegraph*, October 26, 1888.

Full Name: Charlotte Newman • Birth Date: ca. 1830 • Death Date: after February 2, 1892 and before August 1896 • Place of Birth: Virginia • Sex: Female • Race: Black • Places of Residence: Front Royal, Warren County, Virginia; Harrisburg, Pennsylvania: 1726 Walnut Street, 266 Walnut Street. • Connection to the Old Eighth Ward: Husband was a member of the election board of the Third precinct of the Eighth Ward; attended Bethel A.M.E. Church and Wesley Union A.M.E. Zion Church. • Family Members: Husband: Hamilton Newman. Daughter-in-Law: Sarah Newman. Children: Stanton Newman, Thornton Newman, and Felix Newman. Grandchildren: Charlotte Newman Butler, Ruby Newman Moore, and Dr. Felix R. Newman. • Education: No education listed on federal census records. • Occupations: Keeping House. Freedom Seeker (formerly enslaved in Virginia prior to finding freedom in Harrisburg). • Church Membership: Bethel A.M.E. Church. • Activism: Household of Ruth, No. 1 (officer). • Connections: Household of Ruth, No. 1 with Josephine L. Bibb. Joseph B. Popel, Joseph Thomas, John P. Scott, Morris Layton, Sr., William H. Marshall, Benjamin Foote, John W. Simpson, Cassius M. Brown, John Gaitor, and William Howard Day.

A.M./S.M.

SEVENTY
Luther L. Newman

My Contribution: I taught young and adult students so that they might live productive lives as educated citizens. I was dedicated to expanding voting for all African Americans and participated in civic organizations to that end. I advocated that a moving picture showing the execution by hanging of a local African American man at Dauphin County prison not be shown at local movie theaters.

My Legacy: Thoughtful, intelligent, and community-driven, my brief life made lasting change for all those I taught. As an active participant in advocacy for improved lives for African Americans through voting and education, my mission from a century ago is still valid and relevant.

About Me: "Newman has borne himself among us with a courtesy and quiet demeanor that have won the sincere respect of his classmates.... He may well be proud of his scholarship, his ability, in fact, of his entire record at Dickinson [College]." — *Microcosm Yearbook 1911-12*.

"The Colored Voters' Energetic League of Dauphin County adopted resolutions decrying the display of any moving pictures of the hanging of Pascal Hall. Here are the resolutions.... Resolved, That we, the members of the Colored Voters' Energetic League of the County of Dauphin, do vehemently protests against the exhibition of these views, and invoke the aid of all fair and right minded citizens... (Signed) L.D. Kane, C.E. Diggs, L.L. Newman." — *Harrisburg Telegraph,* June 27, 1914.

Full Name: Luther Leon Newman • Birth Date: April 15, 1888 • Death Date: October 19, 1918 • Place of Birth: Harrisburg • Sex: Male • Race: Black (1900 and 1910 Federal Censuses), "Colored" (*Death Certificate*) • Places of Residence: Harrisburg: 615 Forster Street, 147 Linden Street, 26 S. 16th Street. • Connection to the Old Eighth Ward: Resident. Teacher and civil rights activist. • Family Members: Father: Luther W. Newman. Mother: Martha Adelaide (Johnson) Newman. Wife: Kathryn Newman. Grandmother: Anna Johnson. • Education: Harrisburg High School, 1910. Dickinson College, 1912. Courses at Dickinson Law. • Occupations: Charman. Teacher at Allison building. Principal, Springdale Night School. • Church Membership: Capital Street Presbyterian Church. Performed at Bethel A.M.E. Church. • Activism: Iroquois Club,

E. E. Beidleman Republican Club (Secretary), Harrisburg Club of Dickinson College, Colored Voters' Energetic League of Dauphin County. • Connections: Teachers of Morris Layton, Sr. and John P. Scott. Received the Dr. William H. Jones Memorial award in 1908. Attended Dickinson College with James Steward Davis. Esther Popel Shaw, James H. W. Howard.

S.M.

SEVENTY ONE
H. Edwin Parson

My Contribution: My pharmacy was a bustling place that served a diverse community of whites and Blacks. I was involved in local politics and active in forming a YMCA and YWCA for the African Americans of the city. I worked closely with many who loved Harrisburg in order to bring improvements to their lives.

My Legacy: My work with the creation of the YMCA and YWCA for the African Americans of the city had a lasting impact on opportunities for recreation and development. I worked for the strengthening of the African American community through voting and social organizations, which bettered the community for the next generation.

About Me: "He has met with splendid encouragement in his business venture, and enjoys the patronage of both white and colored people." — *Pennsylvania Negro Business Directory*, 1910.

Full Name: Henry Edwin Parson • Birth Date: July 19, 1885 • Death Date: September 28, 1944 (buried in William Howard Day Cemetery, Steelton, Pennsylvania) • Place of Birth: Dublin, Harford County, Maryland • Sex: Male • Race: Black • Places of Residence: Harrisburg: 1162 Cameron Street, 440 South Street, 1104 N. 7th Street, 637 Boyd Street, and 9 S. 16th Street; Philadelphia (pharmacy school). • Connection to the Old Eighth Ward: Resident and pharmacist; business offered a neighborhood social hangout. • Family Members: Father: Isaiah Parson. Mother: Mary A. (Prigg) Parson. Siblings: Lillian C. Parson Wright, Samuel Walter Parson, Mary Parson, Ruth N. Parson Green, Elsie Parson Beckett. Cousin: Irvin Parson. Wife: Fannie/Jennie (Jackson) Parson. Father-in-Law: Richard Jackson; Sister-in-Law: Lizzie Jackson. Children: Sarah Alyce (Parson) Phillips and H. Jackson Parson. • Education: Central High School, 1905. Philadelphia College of Pharmacy, Doctor of Pharmacy, 1908. • Occupations: Pharmacist, Morris' Pharmacy, Atlantic City, New Jersey. Harrisburg Housing Authority. • Church Membership: Bethel A.M.E. Church, Steelton A.M.E. **101** Church. • Activism: Committee to establish the YMCA and YWCA for African Americans in Harrisburg, Sanhedrin Court and Knights of the Round Table, NAACP of Harrisburg (Executive committee), Song Festival committee, Bethel A.M.E. Church, and Dauphin County Afro-American League. • Connections: A. Dennee Bibb, Dr. A. Leslie Marshall, Harry Burrs, W.E. Marshall, Harry Burrs, James H. W. Howard. On committee to plan YMCA/YWCA with Dr. Charles Crampton, Dr. Morris Layton, Jr., C. Sylvester Jackson, James M. Auter, and Walter J. Hooper.

S.M.

SEVENTY TWO
Horace Payne

My Contribution: I was an outstanding student scholar in Harrisburg's Central High School and a graduate of Harvard University. I later returned to Harrisburg to serve my community as a middle school teacher.

My Legacy: I leave the legacy of excellence as the first Black graduate of an institution in Harrisburg to enter Harvard "direct and unconditionally" (*Harrisburg Telegraph*, September 16, 1914). My decision to return to my home community with new knowledge and expertise makes me relevant in a society where discussions continue about the need for educators who are invested in long-term commitment in urban education.

About Me: "Payne stood fifth out of a class of one hundred and seventy-six, and if his record at Central indicates anything, he should have a brilliant record at Harvard." — *Harrisburg Telegraph*, September 16, 1914.

Full Name: Horace Preston Payne • Birth Date: August 1, 1894 or 1895 • Death Date: • Place of Birth: Front Royal, Virginia • Sex: Male • Race: Black (1910 Federal Census); "Negro" (WW1 Draft Registration Card, 1930 *Federal Census*) • Places of Residence: 1411 N. 4th Street, 309 S. 14th Street (1917), and 19 S. 16th Street, Harrisburg, Pennsylvania; 4114 Enright Avenue (1942), and 4232 Cote Brilliant Avenue, St. Louis, Missouri. • Connection to the Old Eighth Ward: Knew many in the community of the Eighth Ward. • Family Members: Father: Richard A. Payne. Mother: Sarah Payne. Siblings: Catherine Payne-Campbell, William Payne, Anna Payne Campbell, Mary Payne Patterson, Robert Payne, and Elizabeth Payne. Wife: M1: Ermille M. Bass, died by 1940; M2: Pauline Ross Payne. Children: Minor P. Payne, Robert W Payne, Catherine Duncan, Horace Jr. Payne and Derek P. Payne. • Education: Central High School, 1912; Harvard University, Bachelor's degree, 1917; Northwestern University, Master's degree. • Occupations: Public School Teacher (Allison and Edison Schools, Harrisburg, Pennsylvania; Sumner High School and Harris Teachers College, St. Louis, Missouri) • Church Membership: Possibly St. Paul's Baptist Church. • Activism: Iroquois Club (1913) • Connections: Catherine Payne Campbell (sister), Jane (Janie) Blalock (fellow teacher), Rev. William H. Marshall (family friend), Cassius Brown, and Dr. A. Leslie Marshall.

Ad.L.

SEVENTY THREE
Catherine Payne Campbell

My Contribution: In my brief time, I served my community as a dynamic teacher in Harrisburg public schools and a committed member of my church. I taught at Calder House for three years and served as a playground instructor before moving to Baltimore.

My Legacy: I served an important role in my community as a dedicated female educator of color.

About Me: "The teachers' training school graduating class will hold its commencement in the high school auditorium this evening.... The teachers will demonstrate their work with the children of the model school. The roll of the 1909 class with the subjects of essays, follows:.... Catherine Payne, 'The Social Life of the Teacher'" — *Harrisburg Telegraph*, May 27, 1909.

"For a number of years Mrs. Campbell was an active member of St. Paul's Baptist Church until she joined the Union Baptist Church at Baltimore." — *The Evening News*, January 5, 1918.

Full Name: Catharine Evelyn Payne; Catherine Payne Campbell • Birth Date: March 16, 1890 (Death Certificate) • Death Date: January 2, 1918 (Death Certificate) (buried in Lincoln Cemetery, Pennbrook, Pennsylvania) • Place of Birth: Virginia • Sex: Female • Race: Black (1910 *Federal Census*), "Colored" (Death Certificate) • Places of Residence: 1411 N. 4th Street, 921 Sarah Street, and 309 S. 14th Street, Harrisburg, Pennsylvania; 1369 N. Carey Street, Baltimore, Maryland. • Connection to the Old Eighth Ward: Knew many in the community of the Eighth Ward, including family friend Reverend William H. Marshall of Wesley Union A.M.E. Zion Church. • Family Members: Father: Richard A. Payne. Mother: Sarah (Polla) Payne. Siblings: Catherine Payne-Campbell, William Payne, Anna Payne Campbell, Mary Payne Patterson, Robert Payne, and Elizabeth Hill Payne. Husband: Dr. David N.E. Campbell. • Education: Central High School, 1907. Teachers' Training School in Harrisburg, 1909. • Occupations: Public School Teacher. • Church Membership: St. Paul's Baptist Church; Union Baptist Church (Baltimore). • Activism: Women's Adult Bible Classes Committee. • Connections: Horace Payne (brother). Harriet Harrison (close friend and maid of honor in her wedding). Rev. William H. Marshall (family friend), Cassius Brown, Dr. A. Leslie Marshall, and W. Justin Carter.

Ad.L.

Photo of a young Esther Popel, future poet of the Harlem Renaissance, upon her graduation from Harrisburg Central High School in 1915. Photo courtesy of Ann and Mary Braxton.

SEVENTY FOUR
Esther Popel

My Contribution: I was an outstanding student at Harrisburg's Central High School and the first woman of color to attend Dickinson College, graduating with high honors. I published my first volume of poetry while still in high school and became a well-regarded poet, writer, and speaker for social justice. I was a life-long advocate for educational equity for Black women.

My Legacy: I left a rich legacy as a teacher, educator, poet, and writer in African American literary communities. My poetry responding to lynching is still widely read today while my other writings, both before and after my involvement in the Harlem Renaissance, receive attention in classrooms today. I am memorialized by the Dickinson College Archives, where my 1919 diary is available for reading.

In My Words:
"'I pledge allegiance to the flag'—
They dragged him naked
Through the muddy streets,
A feeble-minded black boy!
And the charge? Supposed assault
Upon an aged woman!
'Of the United States of America'—"
— "Flag Salute," a poem responding to a contemporary lynching report, Esther Popel Shaw, August 1934.

Full Name: Esther B. Popel; Esther Popel Shaw • Birth Date: July 16, 1896 • Death Date: January 25, 1958 • Place of Birth: Harrisburg, Pennsylvania • Sex: Female • Race: Black (1900 and 1910 Federal Censuses), "Mulatto" (1920 *Federal Census*) • Places of Residence: 703 State Street, Harrisburg, Pennsylvania; Baltimore, Maryland; Washington, D.C. • Connection to the Old Eighth Ward: Resident during childhood; involved in organizations and schools that centered in the Eighth Ward. • Family Members: Father: Joseph Gibbs Popel. Mother: Helen King Anderson Popel. Siblings: Helen Popel, Samuel Popel. Husband: William Howard Shaw, m. April 11, 1925-death in 1946. Daughter: Esther Patricia Shaw. • Education: Harrisburg Central High School, 1915; Dickinson College, 1919; Columbia University, graduate work. • Occupations: War Risk Insurance Department employee. Junior High school teacher in Baltimore and Washington, D.C. for four decades (French, Spanish, English, penmanship, algebra). Playwright. Poet. Speaker in the nation's capital on the theme of race relations; *Negro History Bulletin* editorial board member. Book critic. Ex-officio consultant to Educational Policies Commission. • Church Membership: Wesley Union A.M.E. Zion Church. • Activism: Loyal Temperance Legion; Wesley Union A.M.E. Zion Church; Phi Beta Kappa National Honors Society; Delta Sigma Theta sorority (chair of Vigilance Committee); Washington, D.C. Southeast Settlement House for African Americans (board member); College Alumnae Group (member, vice-president, president); National Association of College Women (charter member, secretary, and constitutional chair, Washington liaison, representative for disarmament petitions). • Connections: Joseph Popel (father), Gwendolyn Bennett, Rosabelle Quann, Jessie Matthews, and W. Arthur Carter.

K.W.M.

SEVENTY FIVE
Joseph B. Popel

My Contribution: I was a life-long resident of Harrisburg who worked for abolitionist causes before the Civil War and fought for Black political and social rights after it. I frequently represented the Eighth Ward as an active member of the local Republican party, serving in leadership positions in political organizations including the Eighth Ward Republican Club and the Eighth Ward Garfield Arthur Club. I planned the celebration of the Fifteenth Amendment for the Harrisburg community.

My Legacy: I was a well-known and well-respected resident and political activist in my community for over 40 years and impacted fellow residents through numerous events and meetings. I helped Black residents of the Eighth Ward to gain access to the vote and to become politically active in the years surrounding the passing of the Fifteenth Amendment.

About Me: "Joseph Popel has been known in this city for upwards of fourscore years as an honest and respectable citizen." — *Harrisburg Telegraph*, February 21, 1881.

"Mr. Popel was identified with every movement tending to the elevation of his race, and was known as a man of broad and liberal views." — Obituary, *Harrisburg Telegraph*, February 19, 1881.

Full Name: Joseph B. Popel • Birth Date: 1820 • Death Date: February 19, 1881 • Place of Birth: Maryland • Sex: Male • Race: "Colored" (Civil War Draft), "Mulatto" (1850, 1860, and 1870 Federal Censuses), Black (1880 *Federal Census*) • Places of Residence: Harrisburg: North Ward, dwelling no. 103 (1850); Ward 4, dwelling no. 458 (1860), **107** Ward 8, dwelling no. 438 (1870), 123 Short Street (1880). • Connection to the Old Eighth Ward: Resident. One of the most politically active members of the community who represented the Eighth Ward in political affairs, especially in conventions and meetings of the local Republican party. • Family Members: Wife: M1: Rachael Popel (1850 *Federal Census*). Wife: M2: Cynthia Popel (1860 and later censuses). Children: Caroline Popel, Margaret Popel, Francis Popel, William Popel, Joseph Popel, Charles S. Popel, Mary A. Popel, and Rachel Popel. • Education: Member of Mr. Alex Sloan's Sunday School Class at Elder Street Presbyterian Church. • Occupations: Laborer. Hotel washer. Public school janitor. • Church Membership: Elder Street Presbyterian Church, Wesley Union A.M.E. Zion Church • Activism: Republican Party (prominent member, who often represented the Eighth Ward as a delegate/committee member);

Garfield and Arthur Club often held in Franklin Hall on South Street (vice president and president pro temp); Eighth Ward Republican Club (president); planner for gala celebrating the Fifteenth amendment; Brotherly Love Lodge (parade chief marshal); Apolia Baseball Club (secretary); Union Republican Central Club (president); Union of Sabbath School Workers. • Connections: John Q. Adams, Cassius M. Brown, T. Morris Chester, William Howard Day, George Galbraith, John Gaitor, George H. Imes, and John W. Simpson.

F.H./A.T.

SEVENTY SIX

Daniel G. Potter, Sr.

My Contribution: My wife and I escaped slavery in Berryville, Virginia during the Civil War by accompanying wounded soldiers to Shippensburg, Pennsylvania. I took great interest in other former slaves and newcomers to Harrisburg and assisted them in buying land and building homes in Verbeketown, a community built on land donated by William K. Verbeke. I was active in the politics of the Sixth Ward and became a prominent man with a large number of friends who stood by me. I was especially dedicated to my Baptist Church and served the community as a deacon and fundraiser.

My Legacy: Through the social, political, and faith-based connections I built in Harrisburg, I left a rich legacy of helping others in my family and community. Vebeketown developed into an important community for African American residents. I was so well known in my time that I was known around Harrisburg as "Uncle Dan."

About Me: "Daniel Potter, one of the leading politicians of the Second precinct of the Sixth ward, and who has been employed about the Capitol grounds for a number of years." — *Harrisburg Telegraph*, November 9, 1899.

"'Uncle Dan', long active in politics and helpful leader to his race." — Article, unknown newspaper, December 1945.

Full Name: Daniel G. Potter, Sr. • Birth Date: December 1, 1842 • Death Date: December 12, 1945 • Place of Birth: Berryville, Virginia • Sex: Male • Race: Black (1900-1920 Federal Censuses) • Places of Residence: Home of George and Ann Massey Pottery in Berrysville, Virginia; 1423 Marion Street, 328 Calder Street, 1325 Marion Street, and 1375 and 1825 N. 4th Street in Harrisburg, Pennsylvania. • Connection to the Old Eighth Ward: Knew many individuals in the ward. • Family Members: Siblings: George Potter, Richard Potter, Matilda Potter Puller. Wife: Betsy Ann (Smith) Potter of Berryville, Virginia. Children: Charles Potter, Elizabeth Potter, Richard Potter, Daniel G. Potter, Jr., George L. Potter, Layton Potter, Elizabeth "Bessie" M. Potter, and Thomas Potter. • Education: No known formal education • Occupations: Harrisburg Car Shop. Day Laborer. Custodian, cleaner, and caretaker on Capitol Hill for over 34 years. Tipstaff in Dauphin County Court. • Church Membership: Marion Street Primitive Baptist Church, member, deacon, and chairman of the Building Committee; Zion Baptist Church. • Activism: Active in Republican politics representing the Second Precinct of the Sixth Ward; nominated for county commissioner; part of committee who organized an event for Black residents of Harrisburg and Steelton about race problems in the region in 1917 • Connections: Roscoe C. Astwood, James M. Auter, A. Dennee Bibbs, Frisby C. Battis, Cassius Brown, Harry Burrs, Charles Crampton, Turner Cooper, C. Sylvester Jackson, Dr. A. Leslie Marshall, Rev. W.H. Marshall, Percy C. Moore, Robert J. Nelson, Luther Newman, Joseph Popel, John P. Scott, and Colonel William Strothers.

M.S.W.R.*

SEVENTY SEVEN

Rosabelle Helen Quann

My Contribution: I was a talented orator and musician who contributed to the intellectual and cultural life of Black Harrisburg as a stellar student and musician. I gave a speech titled "The Evolution of Democracy" at the 1919 Central High School graduation, performed in the 1919 Jubilee, and performed a solo for the Roosevelt Anniversary.

My Legacy: The musical and intellectual communities of Harrisburg, ever-entwined with the Wesley Union A.M.E. Zion Church, still bear my mark.

About Me: "She was a very brilliant girl, very brilliant, and she graduated salutatorian of her class... She was a very beautiful girl, and very brilliant, but college was just out, because there was no money for anything like that for her.... If the old man could have afforded it... of all of 'em in the family she would have been the one to go to college, because she was just so brilliant." — Mr. Robert Quann interview on Black Harrisburg in the 1920's and 1930's, reflecting on his older sister Rosabelle, February 27, 1977.

Full Name: Rosabelle Helen Quann • Birth Date: April 25, 1901 • Death Date: October 17, 1959 (buried in Lincoln Cemetery, Penbrook, Pennsylvania) • Place of Birth: Harrisburg, Pennsylvania • Sex: Female • Race: "Negro" (1930 *Federal Census* and Certificate of Death) and Native American (Source: Robert Quann, interview, 1977, referencing the family's Native American heritage on their father's side). • Places of Residence: 506 South Street (1901-1906), 431 South Avenue (1907-1915), 525 Brown Alley (1916-1921, 1923), 219 Pine Street (1922) in Harrisburg, Pennsylvania; 153 N. Peach Street, Philadelphia (1930); 1213 E. Cumberland Road (1949), Harrisburg. • Connection to the Old Eighth Ward: Lived on Tanner's Alley in the Eighth Ward and belonged to Wesley Union A.M.E. Zion Church. • Family Members: Father: Albert P. Quann. Mother: Annie/Anna Robison Quann, d. April 1923. Siblings: June Quann, Robert Quann, Samuel D. Quann, William Quann, Albert "Rocky" Quann Jr. • Education: Harrisburg's Central High School, 1919 (graduated fourth in class and spoke at commencement); after becoming blind around 1943, took a Dictaphone secretarial course from Thompson College. • Occupations: Domestic (Harrisburg, 1922). Secretary. Waitress (Philadelphia, 1930). • Church Membership: Wesley Union A.M.E. Zion Church • Activism: Served in Sojourner Truth Club of War Camp Community Service; 1,000 Colored Voices; and S.P.Q.R. Society (Latin club). • Connections: Mildred Mercer Cannon, Dorothy Curtis, Mary Braxton Roberts, W. Justin Carter.

S.B.

SEVENTY EIGHT

Aubrey E. Robinson

My Contribution: I was an outstanding student-athlete and sports star at Central High School in both track and football. I was also a talented a student-athlete at Cornell University, where I ran track and studied to obtain a degree in veterinary science. I became a successful veterinarian in New Jersey, where I managed a large animal practice serving especially the dairy farmers that generated milk for nearby New York City.

My Legacy: I broke ground as one of the first African Americans to enter Cornell University College of Veterinary Science, and I was recognized by the university in a 2014 publication. I also mentored my two sons along their journeys to Cornell and to successful careers: one became a prominent veterinarian while the other became a Washington, D.C. District Court judge.

About Me: "Many of you sports followers of the vintage 1912-1913, remember Aubrey Robinson who used to play football for Central High School, and was, at the time, one of the best sprinters in this locality... The Robinson name is being carried along now—by two of his sons—one a member of the Cornell football team, and the other a member of the Big Red Band... the old man is a veterinarian in Madison, NJ." —*Harrisburg Telegraph*, December 5, 1941.

Full Name: Aubrey Eugene Robinson, Sr. • Birth Date: October 24, 1889 • Death Date: January 19, 1962 • Place of Birth: Harrisburg, Pennsylvania • Sex: Male • Race: Black (1900 *Federal Census*) and "Mulatto" (1910 *Federal Census*) • Places of Residence: 10 Haehnlen Street, Harrisburg, Pennsylvania; Ithaca, New York (1916); 15 Walnut Street, Morris, New Jersey; Madison, New Jersey. • Connection to the Old Eighth Ward: Friends with many individuals who lived in the Eighth Ward. • Family Members: Father: Alexander Robinson. Mother: Margaretta Robinson. Brother: Charles A. Robinson. Wife: Mabel Robinson. Sons: Aubrey E. Robinson, Jr., and Charles Robinson. • Education: Harrisburg Central High School; Cornell University Veterinary College, 1920. • Occupations: Teamster for mail wagon (1910). Railroad Worker. Veterinarian. • Church Membership: Unknown. • Activism: Harrisburg Colored Football Team (referee); Rosebud Fountain, True Reformers, No. 78 (secretary) • Connections: Rosabelle Quann, Gwendolyn Bennett, Esther Popel, and Dr. Charles H. Crampton.

Am.L.

SEVENTY NINE

Laura Robinson

My Contribution: In the generation after the American Civil War, I was part of the Benevolent Society, which constructed a monument at Lincoln Cemetery to honor African Americans of Dauphin County who served their country in war.

My Legacy: I left behind an important monument in the region to honor Black soldiers. This lasting monument continues to honor veterans past and present.

Memorable Quotes: "This monument honors Dauphin County African Americans who served in all wars. Its construction was made possible by the Benevolent Society, composed of Jane Chester, Laura Robinson, Catherine McClintock...." — John W. Scott, *African Americans of Harrisburg*.

Full Name: Laura Robinson • Birth Date: September 1850 (1900 *Federal Census*) or ca. 1857 (estimate based on age in 1880 *Federal Census*) • Death Date: November 1904 • Place of Birth: Virginia • Sex: Female • Race: Black (1880 and 1900 Federal Censuses) • Places of Residence: Virginia: 314 Calders Farm, Virginia; Harrisburg: 1184 S. Cameron Street, Harrisburg, Pennsylvania. • Connection to the Old Eighth Ward: Friends of many in Eighth Ward. • Family Members: Husband: Marshall Robinson. Children: Robert Robinson, Liza Robinson, Matilda Robinson, Marshall Robinson, Jr., Harry Robinson, Laura Robinson, John Robinson, Annie Robinson, Henry Robinson, and Rose Robinson. • Education: Could not read or write. • Occupations: Keeping home. Mother. • Church Membership: Second Baptist Church. • Activism: Was part of the Benevolent Society that worked to create a monument for Black veterans in Harrisburg. • Connections: Jane Chester, Catherine McClintock, Benjamin Foote, James Stocks, and Joseph Popel.

L.T./J.R./S.M.

EIGHTY

John P. Scott

My Contribution: I was one of the first two Black students to graduate from the Harrisburg Boys' High School, and I graduated first in my class. I became a dedicated educator who taught at the Calder School and the Wickersham building and served as Harrisburg's first Black administrator. I was also a contributing member to many local chapters of African American political and social organizations, including the Colored Masons, the NAACP, and the Grand United Order of Odd Fellows.

My Legacy: As a committed teacher, principal, and the Harrisburg School District's first Black administrator, I worked as an ambassador for equity in the city. On the day I died, Harrisburg schools closed in my honor. John P. Scott Elementary School on Derry Street still bears my name. My family has continued to invest in Harrisburg education as outstanding teachers and historians.

About Me: "A thirty-third degree charm was presented to J. P. Scott, veteran Harrisburg colored school teacher, at a reception given in his honor... The award was given for meritorious service in this city and the State of Pennsylvania. Mr. Scott probably has done more for colored Masonry in this city than any other man in his generation." — *The Evening News*, November 24, 1920.

Full Name: John Paul Scott, Sr. • Birth Date: December 25, 1859 • Death Date: April 28, 1931 • Place of Birth: Chambersburg, Pennsylvania • Sex: Male • Race: Black (1900 and 1910 Federal Censuses), "Negro" (1930 *Federal Census*), and "Colored" (Certificate of Death). • Places of Residence: 605 South Street (1900, family-owned) and 139 Linden Street (1910, family-owned), Harrisburg, Pennsylvania • Connection to the Old Eighth Ward: Resident. • Family Members: Mother: Rebecca Scott. Sister: Martha R. Scott. Wife: Stella S. Scott, d. June 1916. Children: Rebecca W. Scott, John P. Scott, Jr., Estella H. Scott, William B. Scott, and James L. Scott. • Education: Harrisburg Boys' High School (first salutatorian of color) • Occupations: Public School Teacher in Harrisburg Schools (for 47 years). School Principal. Professor. Orator. Father. • Church Membership: Wesley Union A.M.E. Zion Church (member for 45 years) • Activism: Colored Masons (member), Forster Street YMCA (managing board member), Prince Hall Lodge (Grand Master), St. James Commandery (Grand Commander), and the Royal Arch (High Priest). • Connections: Frisby C. Battis, William Howard Day, James M. Auter, George Galbraith, Dr. William H. Jones, Joseph L. Thomas, William H. Marshall, Morris H. Layton, Jr., and A. Leslie Marshall.

A.M.

EIGHTY ONE
Hannah Scott Cannon

My Contribution: I was a valuable and active member of Harrisburg in the twentieth century who focused my energies on improving, health, safety, and sanitation among the population, and especially the African American community. I contributed my time and talents to supporting, organizing, and teaching about improving the welfare of mind and body.

My Legacy: As an instructional nurse, I impacted and taught many in Harrisburg important skills to improve and sustain a high quality and healthy life. Public health continues to be an area of society that is not equal to people of all races in America. My work was invaluable to the health of my community.

About Me: "At a planning conference at the Phyllis Wheatley YWCA recently... Mrs. Hannah Scott Cannon pointed out the need for greater knowledge in safety, sanitation and disease." — *The Evening News*, October 13, 1945.

"Mrs. Hannah Cannon, of the Visiting Nurses' Association, will speak on 'Health and Race Problems.'" — *Harrisburg Telegraph*, September 4, 1946.

Full Name: Hannah Elizabeth Scott; Hannah E. Williams; Hannah Warrick; Hannah Cannon. • Birth Date: November 29, 1898 • Death Date: February 16, 1995, State College, Pennsylvania • Place of Birth: Philadelphia, Pennsylvania • Sex: Female • Race: Black (1900 and 1940 Federal Censuses), "Mulatto" (1910 *Federal Census*), "Colored" (1926 marriage certificate), and "Negro" (1930 *Federal Census*) • Places of Residence: 1637 Titan Street, Philadelphia, Pennsylvania (1900); 360 Canal Road, Susquehanna Township, Dauphin County (1910); Washington, D.C.; St. Louis, Missouri; 112 Edgecombe Ave, New York City, New York (1930); 232 Liberty Street (1925, 1940-1955) and 233 Liberty Street (1926), Harrisburg, Pennsylvania. • Connection to the Old Eighth Ward: Lived two blocks west of the former Eighth Ward • Family Members: Father: John P. Scott. Mother: Mary Anne (Jones) Scott. Husband: M1: John A. Williams (divorced 1926). M2: Howard Turner Warrick of New York (m. 1926). M3: Thomas L. Cannon (d. April 29, 1955). Children: Caroline (Warrick) Savage, Howard Scott Warrick, and Marian Lillian (Cannon) Dornell. • Education: Central High School, 1918 (graduated with honors). Freedmen's Hospital (a teaching hospital for the Howard University Medical School), Washington, D.C. • Occupations: Registered Nurse. State Nurse. Instructor of Red Cross home nursing classes for mothers/ expectant mothers & home care of the sick. Visiting Nurses' Association. Mother. •

Church Membership: Second Baptist Church. • Activism: Tuberculosis Association (member), Negro auxiliary committee of the Red Cross Disaster Relief Fund Committee, and Educational Committee - Phyllis Wheatley YWCA; YWCA (local speaker), Allison Parent-Teacher Association; local chapter of American Red Cross (instructor). • Connections: Dr. Morris Layton, Jr., Dr. Charles H. Crampton, and Maude Coleman.

S.M.

EIGHTY TWO
John W. Simpson

My Contribution: I had the distinction of being the first African American who ever held a state clerkship position in Harrisburg and worked as a clerk from 1872-75. I served the military in the Civil War and proudly supported my country in times of peace through the GAR and the National Guard. I was active in Harrisburg politics through serving as alderman, and I protected African Americans who wanted to exercise their right to vote after the passage of the Fifteenth amendment.

My Legacy: Together with many of my fellow friends and activists, I encouraged civic participation and involvement in politics for African Americans of Harrisburg. I was also active in improving public school experiences for students, through the creation of the Lincoln Building (later William Howard Day school). I assisted many people to make their voices heard through the ballot box.

About Me: "One of my abiding recollections is of burly Major John W. Simpson mounted on a store box near the polling window at Umberger's Cross Keys hotel.... As the perspiring Major shouted and gesticulated, he generally bore down all opposition and put through all the multitudinous voters he brought to the polls." — J. Howard Wert, Harrisburg *Patriot*, December 9, 1912.

Full Name: John W. Simpson • Birth Date: February 24, 1835 • Death Date: April 7, 1899, from Bright's Disease (buried in Lincoln Cemetery, Penbrook, Pennsylvania). • Place of Birth: Philadelphia, Pennsylvania • Sex: Male • Race: Black (1860 and 1880 Federal Censuses) and "Mulatto" (1870 *Federal Census*) • Places of Residence: Philadelphia, Pennsylvania; Harrisburg, Pennsylvania: 137 Short Street, 133 Short Street, 613 Briggs Street, and 665 Briggs Street. • Connection to the Old Eighth Ward: Resident; political activist and supporter of enfranchisement for African American males. • Family Members: Father: Charles Simpson. Mother: Rebecca Simpson. Siblings: Thomas Simpson, Frances Catto Simpson, Charles Simpson, Mary Ann Simpson, and Rebecca Simpson. Wife: M1: Mary Susan Simpson (d. 1882). Wife: M2: Carrie (Poindexter) Simpson. Child: Marie Antoinette Simpson. Niece: Fanny Simpson. Nephew: Charles Simpson. • Education: Attended public school in Philadelphia. • Occupations: Shoemaker. Clerk, Land office of Pennsylvania, under surveyor General Robert B. Beath. Alderman for Eighth Ward. Organizer, Olympic Baseball Club (1870s-1890s). Father. • Church Membership: Bethel A.M.E. Church. • Activism: Served in Civil War, 24th regiment (sergeant), February 1865 to October 1865; served in 12th infantry (major), National Guard of Pennsylvania; Post No. 520 GAR (organizer and member); served in Free and Accepted Masons of Pennsylvania, Grand Master of Chosen Friends Lodge, No 43, Free and Accepted Masons (grand master); Grand United Order of Odd Fellows, Brotherly Love Lodge, No 896 (member); New Orleans Exposition to exhibit the skill of African Americans of Harrisburg (assistant honorary commissioner). Cato Literary Association (acting member); Pennsylvania Equal Rights League (acting member); and Equal Rights Club of Dauphin County (acting member). • Connections: Josephine L. Bibb, Joseph Popel, George Galbraith, John Quincy Adams, Morris H. Layton, Sr., George Imes, James Auter, Jr., James Stocks, and William Dorsey.

S.M.

EIGHTY THREE
Ephraim Slaughter

My Contribution: I escaped slavery and dedicated myself to a life of service to God, country, and mankind. I fought with the United States Colored Troops in the Civil War for the freedom of all African Americans and had the honor of being the last Civil War veteran living in Harrisburg. I owned multiple properties and cemetery plots.

My Legacy: I am remembered in Harrisburg as someone who served his community. My statue is on display at the National Civil War Museum in Reservoir Park, Harrisburg, and the Ephraim Slaughter American Legion Post 733 is named after me. My estate worht $10,000, which I bequeathed to my widow and her descendants in 1943, would be valued at $148,754.91 today.

About Me: "Slaughter, who escaped from his slave master in North Carolina in 1863 to join the Northern Army, participated in every Memorial Day parade in Harrisburg." — *Harrisburg Telegraph*, February 18, 1943.

"Georgiana and Ephraim Slaughter are both admired for sacrifice and accomplishment, but also for their audacious shared vision to join forces to control their own narrative. They lived the balance of their lives with dignity and companionship, and in time left this world on their own terms and as a more compassionate place than they found." — Dr. Sharonn L. Williams, great-grand-daughter.

Full Name: Ephraim Slaughter (aka Ephraim Newsome) • Birth Date: January 17, 1846 • Death Date: February 17, 1943 (buried in Lincoln Cemetery, Penbrook, Pennsylvania) • Place of Birth: Ahoskie, Herford County, North Carolina • Sex: Male • Race: Black (1880 and 1920 Federal Censuses), "Negro" (1930 and 1940 Federal Censuses), and "Colored" (Certificate of Death). • Known Places of Residence: Ahoskie, Hertford County, North Carolina (1860); 257 Elm Street, Eighth Ward (1880), 903 Grand Street (1900-1930), 612 Briggs Street (1935) and 903 Capital Street in Harrisburg, Pennsylvania (1940). • Connection to the Old Eighth Ward: Real estate investment mentor to peers; used personal properties to shelter family and visitors on short and long-term bases; modeled Christian and philanthropic principles as a community member and local socialite. • Family Members: Wife: M1: Caroline "Carrie" (Grunis) Slaughter, b. South Carolina 1852, m. 1868-1935. Wife: M2: Georgianna Mitchell (Williams) Slaughter, b. West Virginia 1889, m. 1937-1943. Brother: David Slaughter (escaped a North Carolina plantation and relocated to Harrisburg with Ephraim after the war, d. 1892, buried alongside Carrie and Ephraim in Lincoln Cemetery, Penbrook, Pennsylvania). Sister-in-Law: Caroline Slaughter. Niece: Catherine Slaughter, m. John Gaines and relocated to Blair County with only child/ son. Brother: Isaac Newsome—Ahoskie, North Carolina, d. 1921, twice married, two children (John and Eleanor) and fourteen grandchildren, two of whom (Dora Peele and Virginia Hart) visited Ephraim and Georgiana in Harrisburg in 1937. • Education: No formal education. • Occupations: Laborer. Porter. Hotel Employee. • Church Membership: Bethel A.M.E. Church, member and trustee from 1868-1946, assisted in securing financing to payoff the church deed. • Activism: Last Civil War survivor in Harrisburg, Pennsylvania; David R. Stevens Post No. 520 of the Grand Army of the Republic (member); Lodge No. 826 of the Independent Order of Odd Fellows (member); elected to honorary VFW membership; President Franklin Delano Roosevelt's dedication of the Peace Memorial on the Gettysburg battlefield in 1938 (honored guest); served as marshall of several local holiday parades; a well-known citizen who played the role of socialite, informal financial advisor, and mentor in Harrisburg. • Connections: John Q. Adams, James M. Auter, Charles H. Crampton, Maude B. Coleman, Joseph L. Thomas, James W. Grant, George H. Imes, Turner S. Cooper, John Gaitor, C. Sylvester Jackson, and John W. Simpson.

S.L.W.*

EIGHTY FOUR
Susan Sophes Spence

My Contribution: I was an active member of Harrisburg's Eighth Ward. As director of the Martha Washington Association, I organized important social gatherings, including a concert and performance for the Fifth Annual Reunion of Colored People in Harrisburg. As Vice President of the Zion Workers, I hosted a Thanksgiving Dinner to fundraise for Wesley Union A.M.E. Zion Church.

My Legacy: I served my community as a noble governor of the Miriam Household of Ruth, No. 1, one of the most successful lodges of the organization in the country. I donated my time, energy, and financial resources to strengthen Harrisburg institutions, including several schools and Wesley Union A.M.E. Zion Church, a congregation that still thrives today.

About Me: At "the fifth annual reunion of the colored people of Carlisle, Mechanicsburg, Middletown, and this city... The Martha Washington Society, directed by Mrs. Susan Sophes, was present in costume." — Harrisburg *Daily Patriot*, April 21, 1881.

"A Christmas entertainment will be given at Sible & Clark's hall by the Zion Workers of Wesley Union Church. Mrs. Sophes will have charge of the entertainment, which is for the benefit of the church." — *Harrisburg Telegraph*, December 21, 1887.

Full Name: Susan Sophes; Susan Spence (after 1905). • Birth Date: February 8 in 1840-1848 (estimates based on census records and obituary) • Death Date: March 22, 1926 • Place of Birth: Clear Spring, Maryland • Sex: Female • Race: "Mulatto" (1870 and 1880 Federal Censuses) and Black (1900 *Federal Census*) • Places of Residence: Harrisburg, Pennsylvania: 239 Cranberry Avenue (1877-1884), 412 South Street (1900-1901), 217 N. River Avenue (1904-1905), 416 South Street (1908), 702 State Street (1910), 638 Walnut (1911-1912), 816 James Street (1913-1921), 814 Cowden Street (1924), and 817 James (1926). • Connection to the Old Eighth Ward: Resident; work; church; social events. • Family Members: Husband: M1: William Henry Sophes. Husband: M2: Marshall Spence, m. September 1905, d. by 1908. Son: William "Willie" Sophes (adopted), d. March 12, 1889. • Education: Unknown. • Occupations: Keeping House. Janitor (DeWitt Building). Mother. Organizer. Church Woman. • Church Membership: Wesley Union A.M.E. Zion Church (stewardess). • Activism: Martha Washington Association (director), Zion Workers (vice president), Altar Club (president), Wesley Union A.M.E. Zion Church (stewardess), and Miriam Household of Ruth No. 1 Grand United Order of Oddfellows (Noble Governor); donated to Colored Day Nursery. • Connections: William Howard Day, Josephine Bibb, Hannah Jones, Joseph L. Thomas, James Auter, Matilda Stewart, Joseph Popel, John Q. Adams, and Frisby Battis.

A.R.

EIGHTY FIVE
Hattie St. Clair Grant

My Contribution: I was among the earliest African American teachers in Harrisburg's public school district when I taught at the Calder School between 1885 and 1890 and was remembered for my rousing teaching and preparation of children for real life and professional careers. I also contributed to the thriving of Elder Street, later Capital Street Presbyterian Church, as a vocalist and committed church member.

My Legacy: My work in both the local churches and schools of Harrisburg set me apart as a Black woman who consistently invested in my community in spite of societal prejudices at the time. I made a difference in the education of a cohort of African Americans who came of age in the late nineteenth century and the thriving of Capital Street Presbyterian Church, which still exists today. As the mother of seven children, I left my mark in the family ties of the next generation.

About Me: "She was the third Negro school teacher in Harrisburg, and the good she has done will go down in history and be referred to many times in future. Harrisburg had many Negro athletes and baseball players who helped to make Harrisburg prominent, and many of them were given their early school instructions under this popular woman... She was a teacher in the Calder Building and among her early pupils were the Williams and Potter boys, all of whom were prominent in baseball... She was quite a vocalist and manifested much interest in teaching music." — *Harrisburg Telegraph*, February 9, 1943.

"She was the oldest member in years of service and was a member of the choir since she was 14 years old." — Concerning membership in Capital Street Presbyterian Church, *The Evening News*, February 8, 1943.

Full Name: Harriet M. St. Clair; Harriet M. Grant. Nickname: Hattie. • Birth Date: July 2, 1864 • Death Date: February 5, 1943 (buried in Lincoln Cemetery, Penbrook, Pennsylvania). • Place of Birth: Harrisburg, Pennsylvania • Gender: Female • Race: Black (1900-1920 Federal Censuses) and "Negro" (1930 *Federal Census*). • Places of

Residence: Harrisburg, Pennsylvania: 1405 James Avenue, 328 Muench Street (1890-1891), 230 Liberty Street (1893), 228 Liberty Street (1894-1895), 340 Muench Street (1897-1900), 704 N. 7th Street (1902-1907), 130 Balm Street (1908), 1727 N. 7th Street (1909-1911), 128 Balm Street (1913), 303 S. 14th Street (1914), 1326 N. 7th St. (1920), 611 Forster Street (1930), and 1105 Montgomery Street (1943). • Connection to the Old Eighth Ward: Resident; taught near the Eighth Ward at a school that many Eighth Warders attended; Elder Street Mite Society met in the Eighth Ward. • Family Members: Father: George St. Clair. Mother: Mary S. Myers-St. Claire. Husband: James W. Grant, m. 1890-1914, d. September 29, 1914. Sister-in-Law: Clara M. St. Clair. Children: James W. Grant, Jr., Mary L. Grant Braxton, Howard B. Grant, Joseph Louis Grant, Sterling S. Grant, Harriet "Hattie" A. Grant, Mabel Grant Williams (step-daughter). Grandchildren: Joseph N. Braxton, Janice L. Braxton, Lucylle G. Braxton. • Education: Harrisburg High School, 1885. • Occupations: Public School Teacher at Calder School 1885-1890. Mother. Church Woman. Organizer. • Church Membership: Elder Street Presbyterian Church, later Capital Street Presbyterian (member and choir singer for over sixty years). • Activism: Mite Society of the Elder Street Presbyterian Church • Connections: Annie E. Amos, John P. Scott, William Howard Day, Spencer P. Irvin, William H. Marshall, Catherine Payne-Campbell, Harriet Harrison, and James W. Grant.

Al.S.

124

EIGHTY SIX
David R. Stevens

My Contribution: I was a person of deep faith and conviction who deeply influenced my community through church and organizations. I helped establish the Wesley Union A.M.E. Zion Church in Philadelphia and Harrisburg. Under my leadership as minister of the church in Harrisburg, the institution became a place of vital community conversations about race and abolitionism. I also served my country, in the War of 1812 as a drummer boy and in the Civil War as one of the only African American chaplains.

My Legacy: The Wesley Union A.M.E. Zion Church of Harrisburg is still a pillar of the community and hub of important social justice issues. I was remembered for my military service through the renaming of the local GAR Post, which was named David R. Stevens GAR Post 520, est. 1885.

About Me: "In view of the fact that for sixty-two years he has been connected with the cause of God... we deem it fitting as Christians and as citizens to commemorate this unusual fact... and tender to our venerable friend, Elder Stevens, our congratulations that his life, so full of useful service, has been spared even to our time, to bless the church and the world." — A resolution by church members for his Eightieth birthday, *Harrisburg Telegraph*, January 27, 1883.

Full Name: Reverend David R. Stevens • Birth Date: 1803 • Death Date: May 6, 1883 (died in Springdale, buried in Philadelphia). • Place of Birth: Maryland • Sex: Male • Race: "Mulatto" (1860 and 1870 Federal Censuses) • Places of Residence: Philadelphia; Juniper Street, Harrisburg (1880). • Connection to the Old Eighth Ward: Church leader of Wesley Union A.M.E. Zion Church • Family Members: Wife: Harriet Stevens • Education: Learned to read, write, and cipher. Trained as plumber. • Occupations: Plumber. gas and water works. Minister. Army Chaplain. • Church Membership: Wesley A.M.E. Zion Church, Philadelphia (incorporator, trustee, and deacon); Wesley Union A.M.E. Zion Church, Harrisburg; founded churches in Lewistown and Bellefonte, and a mission in Allegheny City (1839). • Activism: Founded Paxton Masonic Lodge, No. 16, which marched in the United States Colored Troops review in Harrisburg on November 14, 1865; served as Chaplain in the 36th United States Colored Troops, 1863-1865; member of Brotherly Love Lodge, No. 896 on South Street. • Connections: Anna E. Amos, John Quincy Adams, John P. Scott, T. Morris Chester, Maud D. Molson, H. H. Garney, O.L.C. Hughes, William Howard Day, George H. Imes, Cassius Brown, Charles Sumner, and Joseph B. Popel.

S.M.

EIGHTY SEVEN
James Stocks

My Contribution: I escaped from slavery in Kentucky and became an influential minister in central Pennsylvania, where I lived the rest of my life. I occupied a number of professions, serving as reverend, superintendent of Sunday schools, teamster, and local express agent. I also fought against the cause of slavery and served my country in the Civil War.

My Legacy: I was thoughtfully involved in Christian education, visiting the imprisoned, and strengthening the A.M.E. church in and around Harrisburg. I had an amazing life seeking and fulfilling the freedoms that all humans deserve, a message still valued today.

About Me: "Rev. Stocks stands high in the estimation of the people of Mechanicsburg, and they hope to see him returned to this charge." — *Harrisburg Telegraph*, May 10, 1887.

"Rev. James A. Stokes is an earnest, consecrated minister who practices what he preaches. He succeeds in all his charges." —*Valley Spirit*, Chambersburg, Pennsylvania, May 26, 1897.

Full Name: James Stocks (only used before 1900); James Stokes. • Birth Date: February 10, 1841 • Death Date: December 31, 1923 • Place of Birth: Warren County, Kentucky • Sex: Male • Race: "Mulatto" (1880 and 1920 Federal Census) and Black (1900 *Federal Census*) • Places of Residence: 217 Meadow Lane (1880), 239 Cranberry Avenue, 120 and 130 River Avenue (1900), and 641 Briggs Street (1920) in Harrisburg, Pennsylvania; Mechanicsburg. • Connection to the Old Eighth Ward: Resident, minister, organizer, and community member. • Family Members: Wife: Ann/Annie M. (Robinson) Stocks. Children: Joseph Stocks, Clara E. Stokes, Frank S. Stokes, Clara E. Stokes, Theopolis Stokes. Grandchildren: Lawrence Stokes, Frank S. Stokes, James A. Stokes. Son-in-Law: Henry Smith. • Education: Mr. Stokes studied for Christian work and was for twenty-six years a traveling elder in his church. • Occupations: Minister. Cook for 9th PA Cavalry, Civil War. Soldier, 45th regiment, US, under Col. Burney, Civil War. Kelker hardware store (Rudolf Kelker was a well-known abolitionist). Teamster. Superintendent of Lochiel Mission Sunday School. Local Express Agent. • Church Membership: A.M.E. charges in Newville and Mechanicsburg, and Baptist Church in West Steelton, Pennsylvania. • Activism: Acted as secretary of group organized to honor Charles Sumner; served in Post 520, GAR; served in cavalry and 45th infantry, Civil War. • Connections: John Q. Adams, George Imes, David Stephens, Jane Chester, Laura Robinson, Catherine McClintock, Benjamin Foote, and Joseph Popel.

126

S.M.

EIGHTY EIGHT
Colonel William Strothers

My Contribution: I was a businessman and entrepreneur involved in politics, social organizations, and business ventures of the Eighth Ward. While I operated businesses ranging from pool halls to dancing schools, I am especially known as a frontrunner in Black baseball. I managed the Harrisburg Giants, the Negro League baseball team in Harrisburg, which would later become one of the first racially-integrated baseball teams in the country.

My Legacy: I was such an important leader in Harrisburg and in Black baseball circles that Cliff Christian, a policeman from Steelton, was referred to as another "Colonel Strothers" as he organized a baseball team in Steelton, the Steelton Giants. I am credited with bringing the Harrisburg Giants from its very beginnings to national acclaim. The Giants played on under different management and different forms until 1955 in Harrisburg.

About Me: "Through his death Harrisburg lost a true sportsman and his death is mourned by a host of friends and baseball fans in the city. In connection with the famous Harrisburg Giants team he gave freely of both his time and money." — *Harrisburg Telegraph,* July 18, 1933.

The Harrisburg Giants came to be known as "the strongest aggregation of Negro baseball stars in the United States, according to general belief." — *Harrisburg Telegraph,* September 20, 1927.

Full Name: Colonel William Strothers • Birth Date: 1868 • Death Date: July 14, 1933 **127** • Place of Birth: Culpepper, Virginia • Sex: Male • Race: Black (1870 *Federal Census*) and "Mulatto" (1910 *Federal Census*) • Places of Residence: According to obituary, moved to Harrisburg around 1888 and lived at: 317 Calder (1896), 322 Calder (1898), 433 South Street (1910), 600 Forster (1914), and 423 Strawberry Street (1920-1930). • Connection to the Old Eighth Ward: Resident; political and community organizer; talesman drawn for the Eighth Ward in 1913; operated pool room and cigar store in the Eighth Ward at 432 South Street; worked in and around the Eighth Ward. • Family Members: Father: Willis. Mother: Mary Ellen. Siblings: Maria Strothers, Rose (Carson) Strothers, Peachie (Thomas) Strothers, Hattie (Higginbottom) Strothers, John Strothers, Joseph Strothers, Willis/William Strothers, Clarence Strothers, Thomas Ware Strothers. Wife: M1: Annie, d. 1897. Wife: M2: Jennie Smith (1870/1880/1930 census). • Education: Unknown • Occupations: Worked at Harrisburg Car Works.

Waiter. Patrolman in the police force (stationed at Third and Market Streets). Pool room proprietor in several addresses in and around the Eighth Ward. Merchant (restaurant at 425 Strawberry). Barber shop. Real estate. Owned a dancing school and operated Felton's Hall. Owner of Harrisburg Giants baseball team. • Church Membership: Wesley Union A.M.E. Zion (funeral); Strothers sold tickets for the American Methodist Episcopal Home Missionary cause. • Activism: Known Republican; Harrisburg Giants professional baseball team (owner and manager); Mutual Association of Eastern Colored Clubs (league commissioner); Chosen Friends Lodge Number 43 F. and A.M. (member); St. James Commandery, No. 17, Knights Templar, B.P.O.E. and the Odd Fellows, Independent, Benevolent, Protective Order of Elks of the World (member); selected as officer of a political club in the Sixth Ward; "Colored Republican Clubs" rally at courthouse in 1916 (chief marshal); Workingmen's Social and Protective Association (founding member). • Connections: Joseph L. Thomas, Sylvester Burris, W. Justin Carter, Daniel Potter Sr., among many others.

An.S.

EIGHTY NINE
James Stuart

My Contribution: I was an influential teacher at the Lincoln School in Harrisburg and principal in York. I served my church as president and treasurer of the Young People's Society of Christian Endeavor of Capital Street Presbyterian Church. I was also known for my abilities as an orator.

My Legacy: I positively influenced a cohort of young children of color in York and Harrisburg and built the faith of my friends through Capital Street Presbyterian Church. That church and the Young People's Society of Christian Endeavor thrive today because of me.

About Me: "The Young People's Society of Christian Endeavor of the Capital Street Presbyterian church held memorial services in the church last evening at 7.15 o'clock in honor of the late James Stuart, who was at the time of his death treasurer of the Harrisburg Christian Endeavor union. Beside being a very active worker in his own society, he took active part in the Christian Endeavor Union and general Christian Endeavor work." — *Harrisburg Daily Independent*, September 29, 1902.

"James Stuart delivered an oration which won him many compliments. His subject was 'No Peace Without Union.' The young man was natural in his gestures, spoke distinctly and gave evidence of more than ordinary oratorical ability in one so young. His ideas were original and commanded the closest attention of the audience." — *Harrisburg Telegraph*, July 1, 1885.

129

Full Name: James Stuart. Alternate Last name: Stewart; Steward. • Birth Date: November 16, 1865 • Death Date: August 25, 1902 (died suddenly in New York City, buried in Lincoln Cemetery, Penbrook, Pennsylvania). • Place of Birth: Harrisburg, Pennsylvania (father arrived in Harrisburg in 1864). • Sex: Male • Race: Black • Places of Residence: Harrisburg, Pennsylvania: 108 Cherry Avenue (1880-1888) and 814 East Street (1900-1902: owned property). • Connection to the Old Eighth Ward: Resident; attended Capital Street Presbyterian Church. • Family Members: Father: Henry Stuart, b. February 3, 1837 in Hagerstown, Maryland. Mother: Eliza Stuart, b. in Maryland ca. 1839. Siblings: Augustus Stuart, Daniel Stuart, Lillie Stuart, Harriet Stuart, and three others. Wife: Mary F. Stuart, b. 1871. Son: James E. Stuart, b. ca.

1894. • Education: Harrisburg High School, 1885 (delivered oration on the theme of "No Peace Without Union") • Occupations: Supervisory Principal of School no. 15 of York, Pennsylvania in 1888. Teacher at the Lincoln School in Harrisburg in 1902. Father. • Church Membership: Wesley Union A.M.E. Zion Church (the church of his father); Capital Street Presbyterian Church (mite society and Young People's Society of Christian Endeavor) • Activism: Young People's Society of Christian Endeavor of Capital Street Presbyterian Church (president and treasurer). • Connections: Anne E. Amos, James H. W. Howard, William Howard Day, John P. Scott, Cassius M. Brown, Theodore Frye, and Morris H. Layton.

S.B.

NINETY
Matilda Stuart

My Contribution: I was a Christian missionary who served as president of the Wesley Union A.M.E. Zion Church Missionary Society. I contributed to the financial and overall well-being of my church and was an activist and organizing member of the Independent Order of the Daughters of Temperance.

My Legacy: I was a dedicated leader of Black Christian organizations in Harrisburg. Wesley Union A.M.E. Zion Church remains a fixture of Harrisburg, thanks in great part to the benevolent work of my life.

About Me: "Special services will be held in Wesley Union African Methodist Episcopal Zion Church tomorrow evening by the Missionary Society in celebration of the fiftieth anniversary of Mrs. Matilda Stuart as an active worker in the society. She has been president of the society for forty-five consecutive years." — *Harrisburg Telegraph*, March 27, 1920.

Full Name: Matilda Bryan; Mrs. Matilda Stuart. Alternate Spellings: Stewart, Steward • Birth Date: October 31, 1843 • Death Date: August 15, 1925 • Place of Birth: Gettysburg, Pennsylvania • Sex: Female • Race: Black (1880-1920 Federal Censuses) and "Colored" (Certificate of Death) • Places of Residence: Harrisburg, Pennsylvania: 418 South Street (1880-1910, owned) and 1511 Derry Street (1917-1925) • Connection to the Old Eighth Ward: Resident and property owner; active member of Wesley Union A.M.E. Zion Church. • Family Members: Father: A. Bryan. Mother: Matilda Lewis. Husband: Jeremiah Stuart. Children: Mary Stuart, Anna "Annie" E. Stuart Davis. Son-in-Law: John M. Davis. Grandchildren: Steward J. Davis, Morris R. Davis, John N. Davis, Dorothy A. Davis, Forrest Davis, Ross O. Davis, Myrtha L. Davis, Matilda A. Davis Fitzhugh, and James M. Fitzhugh (grandson-in-law). • Education: Could read and write. • Occupations: Cook. Mother. Missionary. • Church Membership: Wesley Union A.M.E. Zion Church. • Activism: Active in Wesley Union A.M.E. Zion Missionary Society (president for over 40 years), Wesley Union A.M.E. Zion (stewardess), Wesley Union A.M.E. Zion Church W. H. and F.M. Society, Willing Workers' Club, and Independent Order of the Daughters of Temperance. • Connections: J. Steward Davis (grandson), Mildred Mercer Cannon, Hannah Braxton Jones, Joseph Popel, John P. Scott, Morris H. Layton, Sr., Annie E. Amos, and John Q. Adams.

131

E.S.

NINETY ONE

Annie M. Summers

My Contribution: I was a teacher at the Lincoln building in the Eighth Ward and an activist for virtue as a member of the Independent Order of the Daughters of Temperance.

My Legacy: I was a highly engaged teacher and activist in Harrisburg in social organizations as well as in my church. My role as a well-educated, local Black female teacher in Harrisburg continues to have relevance today amid contemporary conversations about the need for dedicated, local teachers in urban schools.

About Me: "Beloved by all who knew her... Miss Annie Summers, a teacher in the Lincoln building and graduate of the High School class of '91, passed quietly away. She was the leading soprano in the State Street Bethel church choir and an influential member of Samaritan Council, No. 1, Daughters of Temperance. As a teacher she was liked by all, and her many friends will be grieved to learn of her demise." — *Harrisburg Telegraph*, October 25, 1893.

Full Name: Annie M. Summers • Birth Date: ca. 1870 • Death Date: October 24, 1893 (buried at Lincoln Cemetery, Penbrook, Pennsylvania) • Place of Birth: Pennsylvania • Sex: Female • Race: Black (1880 *Federal Census*) • Places of Residence: Harrisburg, Pennsylvania : 1598 Elm Street and 514 Strawberry Avenue. • Connection to the Old Eighth Ward: in charge of the Lincoln school in the Eighth Ward, at the corner of North and Spruce Streets, in the early 1890s. • Family Members: Father: Richard Summers. Mother: Ann Summers. Siblings: Howard Summers, Thomas Summers, Henry H. Summers, Claigett Summers, Clara M. Summers, Sarah E. Summers. • Education: Harrisburg High School, 1891. • Occupations: Teacher. • Church Membership: Bethel A.M.E. Church (leading soprano of choir). • Activism: active member of Good Samaritan Council No. 1, Independent Order of the Daughters of Temperance. • Connections: Annie E. Amos, Josephine Bibb, and Henry H. Summers (relative).

J.S.

NINETY TWO

Henry H. Summers

My Contribution: As a college professor and teacher, I aided the community's commitment to education and self-reliance. Locally, my work in Steelton and Philadelphia specifically sought life improvements for African Americans through education. My life was dedicated to learning and sharing knowledge. I spent most of my career teaching at Wilberforce University, a historically Black A.M.E. institution in Ohio, but was rooted in Harrisburg, returning frequently to lecture and engage in local institutions and the A.M.E. church.

My Legacy: Through extensive education experiences, I devoted my life to the ministry and education of African Americans. I used my own time and energy to ensure that others received quality educational experiences equal to peers. This is still an issue that society continues to wrestle with.

About Me: "Professor Summers… was at the time of his death, professor of Greek and Christian Theology at Wilberforce University, Wilberforce, Ohio. He moved to Harrisburg at the age of 6 and was graduated from the public school here in 1885… He was a member of the American Academy of Political and Social Science; the American Historical Society and the Foreign Policy Association of the Dominican and Haitian Republics." — *Harrisburg Telegraph*, March 8, 1943.

Full Name: Henry Howard Summers • Birth Date: October 12, 1864 • Death Date: March 5, 1943 • Place of Birth: Hagerstown, Maryland • Sex: Male • Race: Black (1880-1920 Federal Censuses), "Negro" (1930 *Federal Census*), and "Colored" (Certificate of Death). • Places of Residence: Harrisburg, Pennsylvania: 514 Strawberry Avenue (1880) and 1604 Elm Street (1900), 139 Linden Street (1943, home of sister-in-law); 1036 Elm Street, Franklin, Pennsylvania (1920); Clifton Pike, Wilberforce, Ohio (1930). • Connection to the Old Eighth Ward: A.M.E. Church • Family Members: Father: Richard Summers. Mother: Annie (Coney) Summers. Siblings: Clayton Summers, Clara E. (Cambel) Summers, Sarah "Sadie" Summers, Thomas Summers, Claigett Summers, and Annie Summers. Sister-in-Law: Sina Summers. Nieces: Gladys Summers, Sarah Summers Waters, Edith Summers. Nephews: A.C. Summers, Jr., Henry Howard Summers, Daniel Summers. • Education: Harrisburg High School, 1885. Professional certificate of teaching, 1892. Howard University, 1910. Oberlin College, 1913. Wilberforce University, Doctor of Divinity, 1924. Ohio State University, 1927. • Occupations: College professor of Greek and Religion at Wilberforce University, Ohio. Coachman (1880). Assistant to Dr. Matthew Anderson, Berean Manual Training and Industrial School, Philadelphia (1913). Pastor, Bethel AME church, Franklin, Pennsylvania (1920). A.M.E. Sunday School superintendent (Lancaster district). Principal of grammar school in Fort Deposit, Maryland. Pastor of college chapel, Wilberforce University (1936). Principal of Hygienic Grammar School, Steelton (1943). • Church Membership: Bethel A.M.E. Church. • Activism: Foreign Policy Association of the Dominican and Haitian Republics, American Academy of Political and Social Science, American Historical Society, Douglass Association for Black graduates of Steelton High School (co-founder). • Connections: Annie M. Summers (sister).

S.M.

NINETY THREE
Joseph L. Thomas

My Contribution: I knew Harrisburg's Black community inside and out as a census enumerator of the Eighth Ward and a trusted undertaker. I was politically and socially active in the community and involved in several social organizations. I co-founded the Masonic Home in Linglestown.

My Legacy: I served an important role in Harrisburg during my time. As an undertaker, I gave numerous Black citizens of Harrisburg the final rites that they deserved in a society divided by the color line, and saw their burial in Lincoln Cemetery and other Harrisburg cemeteries. I also accurately recorded the names, addresses, and important data of my Harrisburg neighbors, strengthening the legislative power of my enumeration district through the U.S. census. My work on the census remains important today, even for the Commonwealth Monument Project, as historians use my information to better understand historic Harrisburg.

About Me: "The praises of Frederick Douglass in the past and of Booker T. Washington in the present have been sounded again and oft for what they have done in improving human conditions. They deserve all the laudations awarded to them. But do not forget that there are men in every community, less known to fame than they, who, unostensiously, are laboring in the same vineyard, and doing the work the Master has given them to do. Harrisburg has had such workers and one of the numbers is Joseph L. Thomas."
— *Harrisburg Telegraph*, May 20, 1911.

Full Name: Joseph L. Thomas • Birth Date: December 16, 1852 • Death Date: March 3, 1913 • Place of Birth: Winchester, Virginia • Sex: Male • Race: Black (1900 and 1910 Federal Censuses), "Mulatto" (1880 *Federal Census*), and "Colored" (Certificate of Death). • Places of Residence: Harrisburg, Pennsylvania: 1326 Fulton Street (1880), 429 State Street, and 26 South Street. • Connection to the Old Eighth Ward: Resident; funeral services for Eighth Ward and elsewhere in Harrisburg; enumerated the population for the federal census. • Family Members: Father: George Thomas. Mother: Martha Coxion. Wife: Marion B. Thomas, m. 1882. • Education: Graduated from a top embalming school in the country. • Occupations: Undertaker. Funeral Director. Waiter at the Bolton. • Church Membership: Elder Street Presbyterian Church • Activism: Grand United Order of Odd Fellows, Colored Masons, Knights Templar, Grand Lodge of F. and A.M. • Connections: John Quincy Adams, Walter Hooper, Millicent Hooper, James Grant.

O.B./K.W.M.

There were few places in Harrisburg more important for Black political organization, business, and social networking in the late 19th and early 20th century than this stretch of South Street between Short Street and Tanner's Alley near the state capitol. The view from the Battis corner (itself associated with Republican politics) shows the drug store owned by H. Edwin Parson (a datestone of 1908 advertises recent refurbishment) and a group of men assembled outside of Colonel Strothers' Pool Hall (Strothers is probably the large man visible in the doorway). Annie Amos, an active crusader for faith, virtuous living, suffrage, and temperance, resided in the same building where she hosted meetings of the Independent Order of Daughters of Temperance. Photo ca. 1913 from Record Group 17, Series #17.522, courtesy of Pennsylvania Historical and Museum Commission, Pennsylvania State Archives, Harrisburg, PA.

NINETY FOUR
Josiah Walls

My Contribution: Over the course of my lifetime, I moved from slavery in Virginia to mayor and congressman in the state of Florida. I served my country by serving in the 3rd regiment of the USCT and then pursued numerous occupations areas over a long career, ranging from politics and law, to publication and farming. My accomplishments and vocations demonstrate the power of perseverance and resilience in the midst of adversity.

My Legacy: Florida A&M College still exists, and the work I did in the Florida Senate and House of Representatives was instrumental in helping to improve education for underrepresented people. I helped to promote Florida nationally and provided aid from the federal government as well. I helped draw the path for underrepresented groups to serve in Congress.

About Me: "Walls spent much of the 42nd and 43rd Congresses advancing the political and economic interests of his Florida constituents. Even Jacksonville's Democratic *Florida Union* praised Walls's efforts on behalf of the state, declaring, 'Mr. Walls adds his mite to what has gone before and does it well.' He affectionately referred to Florida as "my own sunny state," in an attempt to promote the potential of his new home for tourism and farming. Walls presented resolutions for statewide internal improvements including the construction of telegraph lines, customhouses, courthouses, and post offices. He sought funding to improve Florida's harbors and rivers and to create a land–grant state agricultural college. In an 1872 tariff bill, Walls also fought to protect Florida's orchards from foreign competition." — *US House of Representatives: History, Art, and Archives,* **137** Biography on Josiah Walls.

Full Name: Josiah Thomas Walls • Birth Date: December 30, 1842 • Death Date: May 15, 1905 (died in Tallahassee, Florida) • Place of Birth: Winchester, Winchester City, Virginia • Sex: Male • Race: Black (1900 *Federal Census*), "Mulatto" (1863 Enlistment Records) • Places of Residence: Winchester, Virginia (1842-1861); various, forced to work with Confederate Army (1861-1862); Harrisburg, Pennsylvania (1862-1863); military service with Union Army (1863-1865); Gainesville, Florida (1865-1894); Tallahassee, Florida (1894-1905). • Connection to the Old Eighth Ward: Resident of

Harrisburg in 1863; likely knew community in the ward. • Family Members: Wife: M1: Helen "Ella" Fergueson Walls, m. ca. 1864-1885. Wife: M2: Angeline "Angie" Gass Walls (1863-1930), m. 1885-May 15, 1905 (Ella and "Angie" were cousins.) Daughter: Nettie H. Walls (1879-unknown). • Education: Attended school in Harrisburg. • Occupations: Enslaved at birth in 1842. Forced to aid the Confederate Army in 1861. Emancipated by Union forces in Yorktown in 1862. First sergeant and later artillery instructor for Union Army (1863-1865). Mayor of Gainesville, Florida (1865-1870). Congressman (1870-1874: removed twice by white opponent). Lawyer (1873-1884); Newspaper Owner, *Gainesville Independent* (1870s-Unknown). Florida State Senator (1876-1882). Farm Owner (1871-1894). Florida A&M College Farm Director (1894-Unknown). • Church Membership: Unknown • Activism: Republican Party, *Gainesville Independent*, Board of Alachua County Commissioners, and Florida A&M College, among others. • Connections: Unknown.

M.J.

NINETY FIVE
Charlotte Weaver

My Contribution: I was a teacher and advocate of public education. Eventually, I became the principal of the Eleventh Street School.

My Legacy: In my lifetime, I served many students in the hopes of making their lives better. Through education, I hope that the African American children in my segregated school were able to live prosperous lives.

About Me: *"Colored Schools.—Eleventh Street.*—Mixed primary, Charlotte E. Weaver, principal." — *Harrisburg Telegraph*, July 18, 1873.

"Other early African American pioneers in Harrisburg's school district included... Charlotte Weaver (Chester)." — John Weldon Scott, *African Americans of Harrisburg*, 2005.

Full Name: Charlotte Elizabeth Chester; Mrs. Charlotte Weaver. • Birth Date: August 14, 1829 • Death Date: July 8, 1882 (buried in Lincoln Cemetery, Penbrook, Pennsylvania) • Place of Birth: Pennsylvania • Sex: Female • Race: Black (1880 *Federal Census*) • Places of Residence: Harrisburg, Pennsylvania: Ward 4 (1860), 1428 Marion Street (1880), and 305 Chestnut (1878). • Connection to the Old Eighth Ward: Resided near Eighth Ward; knew many involved in Eighth Ward. • Family Members: Father: George Chester. Mother: Jane Mars Chester. Husband: William H. Weaver. Children: Jennie Weaver Palmer, Alda Weaver Brisco, Fannie Weaver Auter, Maggie Weaver Sample, Francis (daughter). Siblings: Thomas Morris Chester, David Chester, Harriett Chester, Ellen Chester, Maria Chester, and Eliza Chester Zedrick. • Education: Unknown • Occupations: Teacher. Principal. Housekeeper. Mother. • Church Membership: Unknown—likely Wesley Union A.M.E. Zion Church. • Activism: Unknown. • Connections: Jane Chester (mother), Thomas Morris Chester (brother), David R. Chester (brother), Amelia Chester, Eliza Zedricks (sister).

139

L.S./S.M.

A distinguished African American gentleman (dis)embarks from a carriage on Fourth Street near State. This man is almost certainly Dr. Charles H. Crampton, who resided at 509 Fourth Street, the exact location shown in this photograph. The growing influence of Black professionals like Dr. Crampton shows how much progress had been made since the day—a half century earlier—when Daniel Webster was arrested by slave catchers at the Harrisburg market.

NINETY SIX

Daniel Webster

My Contribution: I escaped the oppression of slavery to enjoy a life of freedom. Arrested by slave catchers in April 2, 1859 while shopping at the Harrisburg market, I was brought to trial in Philadelphia. Six Harrisburg residents came to testify on my behalf, including Dr. William Jones and notable abolitionists, and some 3,000 people showed up in support. I was acquitted in April 1859, and the city of Philadelphia erupted in celebration.

My Legacy: I left an important legacy about the fundamental value of freedom that generated widespread interest across the Commonwealth in the year before the start of the Civil War. I gained my freedom despite the inequitable Fugitive Slave Act. I generated incredible enthusiasm for abolitionism as Pennsylvania communities of color and abolitionists rallied around my case: witnesses came from Harrisburg to testify, thousands gathered at the courthouse in Philadelphia, others gathered in prayer, and supporters raised $1,000 to purchase my freedom if the judge had not acquitted me.

About Me: "When the commissioner commenced, many sympathizing ladies, who were expecting that Daniel would be sent to Virginia, were 'like Niobe, all tears.' Presently their eyes brightened, as the Commissioner progressed, and when, finally, he ended by saying, in a calm, pleasant way, "The prisoner is being discharged," one wild storm of applause broke it. It was in vain the officers called, or Marshal Yost screamed at the top of his voice. One weak lady with a very strong voice ran to the window and called out,— 'He's free! he's free! Give three hearty cheers!'... A crowd of colored people took hold and paraded him around the streets, as was done to Fanny Ellsler many years ago. The enthusiasm was kept until a late hour of the night—general joy was manifested by his friends at the unexpected result.... For a time we really feared that the man would be smothered by his friends, not less than a thousand whom departed up Fifth street with Daniel borne upon the shoulders of a friend in the middle of the group." — *The Daily Exchange*, April 8, 1859.

Full Name: Daniel Dangerfield (birthname); Daniel Webster. • Birth Date: ca. 1835 (1880 *Federal Census*) • Death Date: Unknown • Place of Birth: Loudoun County, Virginia • Sex: Male • Race: Black (1880 *Federal Census*) • Places of Residence: Loudoun County, Virginia; resident of Harrisburg for 79 years. • Connection to the Old Eighth Ward: numerous friends in the ward. • Family Members: Wife: Rose Webster. Children: Charles Webster and Mary Stroder. • Education: Could not read or write • Occupations: Enslaved at birth. Fence-maker. Laborer. • Church Membership: Unknown • Activism: Unknown • Connections: Dr. William Jones.

A.T.

NINETY SEVEN
Clarence E. Williams

My Contribution: I popularized baseball among the African American community by playing in the national baseball Negro League with the first All-Black Baseball team, the Cuban Giants. I pushed boundaries by playing for what were termed "All-White" teams in the Major League. In Harrisburg, I was the first Black to play for Harrisburg on City Island.

My Legacy: I changed both local and national baseball with my activism as a Black athlete. With the end of segregation and the subsequent integration of major league baseball, my bold strides forward helped to develop baseball into a more equitable sport.

About Me: "While this plucky catcher is fast nearing the half century mark in age, he says he is good for ten years and will continue to play ball until he has to quit. At one time Clarence was on the police force but did not remain long as his love for the National game was stronger than political influences." — *Harrisburg Telegraph*, October 4, 1904.

"A number of years ago Williams was a professional baseball player and was catcher at various times with the Harrisburg Grays, The Cuban Ex-Giants, of New York City, and the Philadelphia Giants." — *The Evening News*, September 28, 1934.

Full Name: Clarence E. Williams. Nickname: Waxey. • Birth Date: January 27, 1866 • Death Date: September 23, 1934 in Atlantic City, New Jersey (buried in Atlantic City Cemetery). • Place of Birth: Harrisburg, Pennsylvania • Sex: Male • Race: Black (1900-1920 Federal Censuses) and "Negro" (1930 *Federal Census*) • Places of Residence: Harrisburg, Pennsylvania: 1331 Wyeth Avenue (1900), 661 Sayford Avenue (1910-1930), 335 Calder Street, and 1328 Fulton Street. • Connection to the Old Eighth Ward: Lived three blocks north of Eighth Ward; played baseball with many Eighth Warders. • Family Members: Siblings: Newton Williams, Robert Williams, Mrs. Lillie Williams Crummel, and Mrs. Eliza Williams Alexander. Wife: Helen (Harris) Williams, b. April 1876, m. April 2, 1891. Children: Mary E. Williams Fountain (b. 1892), Clarence Williams (b. 1894), William A. Williams (b. 1898), Helen Williams (b. 1901), Edith M. Williams (b. 1904), Ethel Williams Blackwell (b. 1908), and Hilda Williams Felton (b. ca. 1914). • Education: Unknown • Occupations: Policeman sometime before his baseball career began in 1887. Baseball Player (1887-1913). Father. • Church Membership: Unknown. • Activism: Unknown. • Connections: Colonel Strothers (baseball), William C. Williams (father).

M.J.

NINETY EIGHT

William C. Williams

My Contribution: As a former enslaved person who found freedom in the north, I worked to assert those freedoms in Harrisburg. I helped my community as the first African American patrolman in the city. I also served on political committees to ensure that voters' voices were represented at the polls.

My Legacy: As a patrolman, I protected residents so they could live peaceably. I encouraged many citizens to use their Fifteenth Amendment rights to ensure voice and representation in voting. These actions worked towards a better life for citizens in Harrisburg.

About Me: "William C. ('Uncle Bill') Williams, born a slave on a Virginia plantation, whom the fortunes of war brought north to this city during the retreat of General Banks in the Civil War....became a hod carrier in this city until he was appointed as the first Negro city policeman by Mayer Cameron Wilson. He later became chief contractor in unloading coal boats that plied the canal from Steelton... Fifty years ago 'Uncle Bill' helped the late Danie H. Potter found the Zion Primitive Baptist Church" — *Harrisburg Telegraph*, Aug 6, 1927.

Full Name: William C. Williams. Nickname: Uncle Bill. • Birth Date: May 1838 (1880 and 1900 *Federal Census*), 1839-1840 (1910 and 1920 *Federal Census*), 1848-1850 (death certificate and obituary) • Death Date: August 5, 1927 (buried in Lincoln Cemetery, Penbrook, Pennsylvania) • Place of Birth: Fauquier County, Virginia on plantation of Colonel Joseph H. Hoerner • Sex: Male • Race: Black (federal censuses) and "Colored" (marriage and death certificates) • Places of Residence: Fauquier County, Virginia; Harrisburg, Pennsylvania: Sixth Ward, 1408 Marion Street (1883), 335 Calder Street (1892), 1333 Margaret Street (1900), 1337 James Street, 1314 Marion Street (1899), and 1332 Williams Street (1910-1927). • Connection to the Old Eighth Ward: Resided several blocks north of Eighth Ward; knew Eighth Warders. • Family Members: Wife: M1: Jennie (Smith) Williams. Wife M2: Elizabeth "Eliza" Trummel Williams, m. 1900-August 5, 1927. Siblings: George Williams. Children: Shelly Williams, James Williams, Elmer Williams, Clara Williams, Mary Williams, Clarence "Waxey" Williams, Robert M. Williams, Newton Williams, Mrs. Lillie Williams Crummel, George Williams, Pear Williams (adopted), Carrie Williams Brown, Mrs. Eliza Williams Alexander, Alverta Woodson (step-son), Lester Woodson (step-son). Grandchildren: William D. Williams. • Education: Could read and write • Occupations: City Policeman, appointed in 1883 by Mayor Cameron Wilson. Laborer. Street sweeper. Hod carrier, construction. Contractor, unloading coal boats. Janitor, Calder School building. • Church Membership: Zion Primitive Baptist Church on Marion Street (founding member, treasurer and deacon). • Activism: served as Member, Grand United Order of Odd Fellows, No. 896; active in Republican politics. • Connections: George H. Imes, John W. Simpson, Clarence Williams, and Daniel H. Potter.

O.B./S.M.

NINETY NINE
John H. Wolf

My Contribution: I was a leader of Harrisburg's Underground Railroad network. I was the first African American teacher in West Chester, Pennsylvania, and brought that skill of teaching young pupils to Harrisburg. I was an advocate of reforms for African Americans, which included their liberation both domestically and in Liberia.

My Legacy : I improved the lives of others by putting my own security at risk. I valued freedom and worked for others to have the freedoms of their mind through education and body through freedom from slavery. As one of many, I changed many lives, through education and freedom. Through personal risks to safety and pushing social norms, my efforts had a rippling effect on many.

About Me: "While in Harrisburg, he cooperated with Garrison, Douglass, and Lewis Hayden in helping fugitive slaves to make their way to Canada. He was sometimes away from home for days helping the slaves to the next safe place in the "underground" system and has often amused his family by relating some the hair breadth escapes which he had from the owners of the fugitive slaves. He was president of that portion of the underground system in Pennsylvania."
— *Boston Globe*, February 8, 1899

Full Name: John H. Wolf. Alternate spellings: Wolfe and Wolff. • Birth Date: November 1817 • Death Date: February 7, 1899 in Boston • Place of Birth: Chester County, Pennsylvania. • Sex: Male • Race: "Mulatto" (*1850 and 1860 Federal Censuses*) • Places of Residence: West Chester, Pennsylvania; Columbia, Pennsylvania; East Ward (1850) and Fourth Ward (1860), Harrisburg, Pennsylvania; 17 Phillips Street, Boston (1900). • Connection to the Old Eighth Ward: Underground Railroad. • Family Members: Father: Aaron Wolf. Mother: Annie Bostick Wolf. Wife: Mary (Taylor) Wolf. Children: Harry Wolf, Bertha (Wolf) Cook, Mary (Wolf) Robinson, Josephine Wolf, Cora (Wolf) Bruce, Mary Wolf, Wendel Wolf, Edmund Wolf. • Education: Unknown. • Occupations: School teacher in Boston and Cherry Alley in Harrisburg. Book writer/seller. Founder/editor of *New Republic and Liberian Missionary Journal.* Underground Railroad conductor. Recruiter of African Americans for the Civil War. Father. • Church Membership: A.M.E. Churches (associated with many, but specific churches unnamed) • Activism: State Convention of Colored Citizens of Pennsylvania (representative), 1848; founded first lodge of colored Odd Fellows (Brotherly Love) in Harrisburg; first Black man to teach in West Chester, Pennsylvania. • Connections: Zacariah Johnson, Aquilla Amos, Thomas Morris Chester, Harriet McClintock Marshall (fellow activist in UGRR), Joseph Cassey Bustill (UGRR), Jane Chester (UGRR), Mary Bennett (UGRR), and William Jones, Sr.

145

S.M.

ONE HUNRED
Eliza Zedricks

My Contribution: I hosted numerous events in my home, 305 Chestnut St, the home I grew up in and inherited from my mother, Jane Chester. After my mother's death, I continued her tradition of hosting important guests traveling through Harrisburg, as well as offering my home for organizing. One of those meetings was the launch of St. Augustine's Episcopal Church, which later became Church of the Holy Cross, then St. Gerald's Episcopal before it merged with St. Paul's Episcopal Church today.

My Legacy: I was one of the founding members of St. Monica's Guild/St. Augustine Episcopal Church (1906), later Church of the Holy Cross. Tollie Caution went on to become the first African American to serve the national Episcopal Church as Secretary for Racial Ministries, which later became Union of Black Episcopalians. Today, Central Pennsylvania's Nathan Baxter Chapter of the Union of Black Episcopalians continues the work envisioned by the group that gathered in my home. St. Paul's Episcopal Church's recently dedicated St. Augustine's chapel stands as a commemorative symbol of our work in the community.

About Me: "In June 1906, the Rev. Mr. Livingston came to Harrisburg to make his survey. On June 12, a meeting was held at the home of Mrs. Eliza Zedricks, 305 Chestnut Street. At this meeting the Rev. Livingston spoke and urged organization of St. Monica's Guild."
— *The Evening News*, June 14, 1941.

Full Name: Eliza Chester Zedricks • Birth Date: 1846 • Death Date: October 30, 1918 • Place of Birth: Harrisburg, Pennsylvania • Sex: Female • Race: Black (1850-1910 Federal Censuses) • Places of Residence: 305 Chestnut Street (property owner), Harrisburg, Pennsylvania; Carlisle, Pennsylvania (1880's). • Connection to the Old Eighth Ward: resided two blocks southeast of the Eighth Ward; founding member of St. Augustine Church, located at 433 North Alley. • Family Members: Father: George Chester. Mother: Jane Chester. Siblings: Thomas Morris Chester, David Chester, Charlotte Chester, Maria Chester Booth, Harriet Colbert. Husband: John Zedricks. Children: Harry H. Zedricks, Chester W. Zedricks, Grace Minerva Zedricks Winters, and Bertha F. Zedricks. Daughter-in-Law: Rhoda Zedricks. • Education: could read and write • Occupations: Hairdresser. Janitress (Stevens building). Glove Cleaner (1910). Mother. • Church Membership: Wesley Union A.M.E. Zion Church; Capital Presbyterian Church; St. Augustine Episcopal Church (founded in 1906). • Activism: Thursday Club, St. Monica's Guild, Bachelor Maids. • Connections: John Q. Adams, Frisby C. Battis, Morris H. Layton, Sr., James H. Howard, T. Morris Chester, Jane Chester (mother), David R. Chester (brother), and Charlotte Chester Weaver (sister).

I.S./J.T.C.